AMERICA ON SIX RUBLES A DAY

AMERICA ON SIX RUBLES A DAY

or
How to Become a Capitalist Pig

YAKOV SMIRNOFF

VINTAGE BOOKS

A Division of Random House
New York

A Vintage Original, November 1987
First Edition

Copyright © 1987 by Comrade in America, Inc.
Illustrations copyright © 1987 by Lois Lowenstein
Interior photographs copyright © 1987 by Edward Sanderson

Library of Congress Cataloging-in-Publication Data

Smirnoff, Yakov, 1953–
America on six rubles a day.

"A Vintage original."
1. American wit and humor. 2. United States—Social
life and customs—Anecdotes, facetiae, satire, etc.
I. Title.
PN6162.S536   1987   818'.5402   87-40072
ISBN 0-394-75523-5 (pbk.)

MANUFACTURED IN THE UNITED STATES OF AMERICA

10 9 8 7 6

Book design by Carole Lowenstein

To my mom and dad. They arrived here in America as strangers, not even able to read their new passports. Now, after many years of struggle, they stand on their own feet and take charge of their lives. For people in their golden years, it isn't easy to learn a completely new way of life. I admire their fight for survival . . . and celebrate their victory.

I dedicate this book to my parents, who, I'm proud to say, can now read it.

Thanks to Mike Scully and Brian Scully
for helping me write this book.

Acknowledgments

I'd like to thank Mitzi Shore, owner of the Comedy Store, who once said, "Stay in Hollywood because there is always a place for someone who is good and different." Then she immediately sent me on the road.

And I'd like to thank my wonderful agent Bob Williams, who put this book deal together, and only charged me 65 percent.

Contents

Introduction

Who Is This Book For?

You!

Whether you are like me, and left the Soviet Union to escape political oppression; or whether you're from England and moved here to see London Bridge and the *Queen Mary;* or whether you left France to escape Jerry Lewis movies; or whether you left Japan to escape from Godzilla and Rodan (and Jerry Lewis movies); or whether you're just from a culturally deprived place, like Cleveland . . . this book is for you.

America is a wonderful but sometimes confusing country. If this book of my experiences and observations makes just *one* person's adjustment to life in this country easier, or enables just *one* American to see his land through the eyes of an immigrant, then I'm going to have an awful lot of these books left over in my closet.

AMERICA ON SIX RUBLES A DAY

"Funny, she looked taller on TV."

BECOMING A CITIZEN

or

Sworn in the USA

So you want to become an American citizen. Well, I think that's a great idea, but there are a few things you should know first. You have to wait five years before you can apply for citizenship, and then you have to pass a test on some general history of the United States. If that makes you nervous, do what I did and pretend that you're answering questions on a game show. If you answer them wrong, though, you'll be going home with luggage. (Your own!) But if you answer them correctly, you'll win and become a citizen. Just don't get carried away like I did, and try to trade your citizenship away for what's behind door number 3.

July 4, 1986, is a date I'll never forget. It was then that the Statue of Liberty ceremonies were held at Ellis Island and I was sworn in as an American citizen. Now, no matter on what date you become a citizen, it will be a thrill like none you've ever had before. It was a double thrill for me because I was chosen to represent California at the ceremony. I felt like Miss America.

(Then again, a lot of guys in California feel like Miss America.)

After taking the oath, I looked around at the smiling faces of all the immigrants near me, and only one thought came to mind: "I hate those goddamn foreigners who come over here and take our jobs!" I'm kidding, of course. Actually, my first thoughts were about how my life would change now that I was an American. Would I lose my accent? I hoped not, because then I wouldn't qualify to manage a 7-Eleven store or win the California Lottery.

Then came the unveiling of the newly renovated Statue of Liberty. Like a lot of you, I hoped that they hadn't modernized her too much. I momentarily pictured her in green Reeboks, or, instead of holding a torch, she'd be flicking a Bic. But my worries were for nothing. She was as beautiful as ever, and I couldn't take my eyes off of her. I was oblivious to everything around me; it was like I was in a trance. When someone told me that the last ferry was leaving, I said, "Good, let him go." I missed the boat, then realized that I had no way to get off the island. I suddenly knew how Gilligan must have felt.

Fortunately, I was not alone. Several FBI agents, for security reasons, were spending the night on the island. We huddled around a campfire and when things started to get a little boring, I taught them some songs I remembered from the years I spent as a child in Russia at winter camp. We sang "Please Release Me, Let Me Go," "Staying Alive," and "These Boots Are Made for Marching." Then we played some games like I've Got a Military Secret. We were actually having a lot of fun until I asked a couple of the FBI guys to pose for some pictures with me. All of a sudden, they scattered in all directions. Somebody then told me that FBI agents are not allowed to be photographed. This is a great tip for someone new to the country:

if you're being chased by the FBI, you don't need a gun—just whip out an Instamatic. They yell, "Freeze!," you yell, "Cheese!"

Later on, as everyone was falling asleep, I started to think about all the exciting things in my life. Before I knew it, I was falling asleep too, so I started to think about Burt Reynolds' life instead. Awake again, I thought about how much my life had changed since I came to this country. Why, just a few years ago, I was living in Russia in a crowded, cold apartment, always being watched by the KGB. But now I was in America, sleeping outside surrounded by forty FBI agents. What a country!

I don't know how hard it was for some of you to leave your country, but in my case, getting out of Russia was not easy. I applied for a visa, but they gave me a MasterCard. Actually, there aren't any such things as credit cards in the Soviet Union, not even American Express. They do, however, have Russian Express—"Don't leave home!" And the government makes leaving very difficult. While my application was being reviewed, they investigated me, got me fired from work, and turned all of my friends against me. It was like being on "60 Minutes."

Like you, I remember the day I arrived in the United States. I had read stories that said the first thing every immigrant sees is the Statue of Liberty. What I didn't realize is that those people came by boat. I flew into Kennedy Airport. I looked all over for the statue. Finally, at the immigration office I saw a four-hundred-pound lady in a green dress. I said to her, "Are you the Statue of Liberty?" She answered, "No, but I'm tired and I'm poor."

Yes, that was a little disappointing, but then I saw something that told me this was the place for me. It was a large billboard and it had my name on it: "Smirnoff . . . America Loves Smirnoff!" America and her people made me feel wanted. In Russia I was wanted, but it wasn't quite the same feeling. Now that I am a citizen of this great country, it makes me proud to think of myself as one of America's people. Right after I was sworn in, I felt like I'd just been given a lifetime membership to the greatest country club in the world.

America. What a country!

"This iron must be defective."

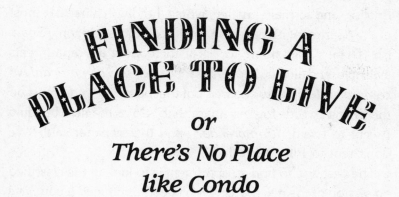

2

FINDING A PLACE TO LIVE

or
There's No Place like Condo

When you first arrive in the United States your thoughts will be of Life, Liberty, and the Pursuit of a Nice Apartment. That would be happiness enough for me, because in Russia we had to live in communal apartments, with five families all using the same kitchen and bathroom. For twenty-six years, I shared the same bedroom with my parents. To say the least, it was awkward. When I was a kid, whenever my parents wanted to make love, my father would tell me to go look out the window. Once while I was looking out, he asked me, "What can you see?" I told him, "Our neighbors making love." He said, "How can you tell?" And I answered, "Because their son is looking at me!"

Needless to say, when my parents and I came to New York, getting a nice, large apartment was a big priority. Now, if any of you reading this are also trying to get settled in the Big Apple, let me give you some advice. If you don't speak the language, save yourself some time and take along an interpreter. The problem I ran into was that I couldn't speak any English, and to make matters worse, I didn't realize that most of the apartment managers in New York City speak only Spanish. There I was, trying to ask if there were any apartments available, and all they kept answering was, *"No comprende! No comprende!"* Finally, I figured out that *no comprende* must be the English words for "no apartment." So at the next building I went to I said, *"Comprende?"* and the manager said, "We don't rent to Puerto Ricans."

The best way to find an apartment is to look in the classified ad section of the newspaper. Don't get discouraged if you have a little trouble understanding what some of the ads mean. I had difficulty with them at first, but now I'm an expert. For example, you may wonder what they're talking about when they say that an apartment has one and a half bathrooms. That confused me too, until I read somewhere that the average American family consists of 3.5 people.

As you can see, I've become quite an authority on the subject. What's really so surprising is how complicated it can be getting an apartment in the United States. Here you have to deal with things like references and security deposits. In Russia, it was much simpler. You didn't need any references, and for a security deposit, they made you leave your grandparents. If you stained the carpet . . . they kept your grandparents.

Finally, after much searching, my parents and I found a nice place to live. We had no sooner gotten through the door than my dad noticed the incredible view we had of the New York skyline. He said to me, "Son, look out the window!" And my mom hollered from the bedroom, "Not tonight, I have a headache."

Like many people who come to the United States from another land, we arrived with little more than the clothes in our suitcases. After moving into our apartment, I think we may have had about $100 between us, and no furniture and no food. That first night in our new home we were all a little depressed, and my mom was sitting on her suitcase crying when we heard a knock at our door. Since we didn't know anyone in America, we got very scared. What if it was robbers, or the KGB, or something even worse—a Jehovah's Witness. When we opened the door, we were really surprised. It was all the other tenants of the building come to welcome us. It seems that they were all immigrants themselves originally, and they wanted to help make us feel at home. It was very warm and touching, and it reminded me of one of those nice old black-and-white Jimmy Stewart movies . . . before Ted Turner got hold of them.

Our neighbors were so good to us, and they all brought gifts. One man knew that we didn't have any furniture, so he gave us one of those La-Z-Boy chairs that vibrate. My parents thought it was a wonderful gift until my mom spotted the cord coming out of it. It scared the hell out of her and she said, "Why do they want to give us the electric chair? We paid the security deposit." Then the man plugged in the chair and showed us how it vibrated. My parents loved it, particularly my mom. Since we didn't have a blender, she'd sit in it with some food and put the vibrator on High. We haven't been able to get my mom off of that chair. I recently offered to buy her a blender, but she said no, she'd prefer a new chair with a Puree setting.

We received many other nice presents that night. Someone else gave us a waffle iron and I ruined three pairs of my pants with that damn thing. For a month, I was walking around with that waffle-butt look. They also brought a dishwasher . . . and he was a pretty nice guy.

I hope that a lot of you are lucky enough to have good

neighbors, like we did. But even with all the help that others may give you, it will still take some time to get settled in. In my situation, I had to think about things that we never even had to consider while living in the Soviet Union. I had to buy apartment insurance here, and it was very expensive. In Russia, nobody owns anything worth insuring, but at least the premiums are reasonable. Once we had everything moved in, even the simplest tasks were difficult for us. For instance, when we went to buy wallpaper, we were overwhelmed by the assortment of colors and patterns available. It would never be such a difficult choice in the USSR. There you would buy whatever the store had and be happy with it—because there wouldn't be any gay decorator to tell you, "It'll never work."

Once you have your apartment and you're all moved in, the last important thing you'll need to do is get a telephone. For me, this was quite a surprising experience, because it was so easy and so fast. In the Soviet Union, when we called to make an appointment to have a telephone installed, they told us to stay home between 1963 and 1976. The Russian phone company is very different from the American one. When you call "information" there, two guys come over and get it from you. They have television commercials that say, "Reach out, interrogate someone." And instead of Yellow Pages, they have Red Pages . . . "Let your fingers do the marching!" To be perfectly honest with you, I much prefer A.T.&T. to K.G.&B.

Now, when you order your phone service in America, you must be prepared to make some decisions. When I placed my order, the clerk asked, "Do you want a party line?"

I answered, "No, that's why I left the Soviet Union."

Then she asked, "Do you want call forwarding, call waiting, or three-way calling?"

I said, "I just want to call."

Finally I got my phone installed and the very first call I received was from Russia. They said, "We've got your number."

One of the more interesting services that you can get through your telephone is "phone sex"—and they have their own version of "three-way calling." These are special numbers that you can dial for sex, and some girl talks you through it. When I first heard about this service, I thought to myself, "What a country!" What I didn't know was that they charge you two dollars every time you call. My first month's phone bill was for $1,400. The phone company did to me what I wanted to do to that girl!

OUR FIRST NIGHT IN AMERICA, WE HEARD A KNOCK AT THE DOOR AND WE GOT SCARED. WHAT IF IT WAS THE KGB OR SOMETHING EVEN WORSE—A JEHOVAH'S WITNESS!!

"Individually tested? I want that job!"

3

FINDING WORK

or
Take This Job and Shove It

One of the biggest surprises I got when I moved to the United States was how hard it is to find a job. In the Soviet Union there is no such thing as an unemployment problem. All you have to do is pick up a Russian newspaper and you'll see that there are many openings available, for suspects . . . inmates . . . targets. (They aren't sticklers for previous experience either.)

Like many people, you probably came to America without much money, which means you'll have to do some pretty clever planning. I would like to suggest that you use this three-step program for financial success. First, evaluate your skills and qualifications to accurately gauge your career options. Second, analyze the current trends in the employment market to discover your hiring potential. And third, sponge off a rich person for as long as possible. Or do what lots of Americans have done—marry and divorce Johnny Carson.

Now, it wasn't that easy for me. I had a very hard time finding work in the beginning because I couldn't speak the language well, and I know that cost me a few jobs. You see, the first job I was offered was in New York selling drugs . . . for four dollars an hour. Naturally, I turned it down, because I knew what drugs were. I just wish I had known the meaning of "at the pharmacy."

Being unable to communicate effectively and be clearly understood will get you automatically rejected from most jobs, with the possible exception of politician, where it's a basic requirement. If you still have trouble with English, I would suggest that you either look for a position where you can remain silent (like national security advisor) or find one where you can learn the language through the conversations you'll be having with the general public. And I found the perfect job for that: bartender. Thanks to the help of many of my customers, I picked up the language very quickly. Unfortunately, though, I learned to speak English by slurring my words and falling off bar stools. (A difficult way to go through life, unless you're Ed McMahon.)

Of course, getting a bartender's job is not easy. First you have to find a bar with an opening. The fellow I replaced was an American Indian, and the reason they fired him was that every time someone asked for a Manhattan . . . he'd charge them twenty-four dollars. During the interview for a bartender's job, be prepared, because the bar owner is going to ask you several questions to determine your qualifications. In my case, the first thing he asked me was if I knew how to mix up a Grasshopper. I answered, "Sure, just blindfold him and turn him around five times fast." The next thing he asked me for was a Black Russian. I said, "What's happening, comrade!" Then he told me to get him a Bloody Mary. I did, but boy was Mary mad. I was grateful he never ordered a Harvey Wallbanger. Finally he asked me if I knew how to make the perfect Manhattan. I replied, "Absolutely, just clean up all the garbage!" I got the job. And for a while, the money was great.

You see, the bar was in Washington, D.C., and I used to get a lot of business from the Pentagon. I really loved waiting on those air-force generals because they would pay $800 for a Screwdriver. Then one day the owner changed my hours and told me I'd be working the graveyard shift. I thought to myself, "Wow, a bar in a cemetery. What a country! Talk about your 'last call'!" During Happy Hour the place must be dead!

Even though jobs are sometimes scarce, you can find them if you're willing to go out and work. I've had many different jobs and have been working since I was a child in the Soviet Union. I remember I used to be a Russian newspaperboy, but I ended up quitting because they kept expanding my route. I got tired of riding my bike through Poland and Czechoslovakia. And I really used to hate collecting in Afghanistan! The Communist party gives everyone in the Soviet Union a job, but then they don't want to give the people any money. However, nobody's complaining, because they found the perfect compromise. The Russian government pretends that they're paying, and the people pretend that they're working.

Because there is no incentive in the USSR, the service you get is usually slow, inefficient, and rude. (It's a lot like a trip to the Department of Motor Vehicles here.) Depression may explain why there is so much absenteeism due to alcohol abuse in the Soviet Union. The Russian government is really clamping down on the sale of alcohol in an attempt to solve the problem. I understand that they recently increased the minimum drinking age there—from two to four.

I heard a story about Mr. Gorbachev visiting a factory just outside of Moscow. He was concerned about the alcoholism problem and he asked a worker, "Do you think you could come to work if you'd drunk one glass of vodka?"

The worker said, "Yes."

Gorbachev then asked him, "Do you think you could come to work if you'd drunk two glasses of vodka?"

The worker answered, "Probably."

Gorbachev finally asked the man, "Well, do you think you could still come to work if you'd drunk three glasses of vodka?"

The worker replied, "I'm here, aren't I?"

Naturally there are problems in the employment market here in the United States too. Alcoholism. Financial scandal. Sexual depravity. These are just some of the things you may have to deal with on the job—but then no one said you *had* to work for the PTL Club.

America is truly the land of opportunity. Just look through the help-wanted section of your local newspaper. There are jobs for just about everybody. I saw an ad recently that said, "Part-time Woman Wanted." I thought to myself, "What a country! Even transvestites can get work."

If I can give you one tip: don't believe everything that you read in the paper. When I first arrived in the U.S. I was told that the newspaper was the best place to find a job, but no one ever told me that I should be looking in the classified ad section. I ended up looking on the front page and saw the headline BANK ROBBER WANTED BY FBI. I thought to myself, "What a country!" So I called the FBI. They said that the pay wasn't very good, but at least I'd be able to make my friends personalized license plates for Christmas. I turned that one down.

Finally, you should be aware that some of the very best jobs are never advertised. For example, have you ever seen a package of condoms? Each package says that it's been "pre-tested."

Now, I only have one question. How can I get that job? (I'll bet that the competition must be pretty stiff.) I can see one drawback to this type of work. It's probably the only job in the world where a headache could be considered a career-ending injury.

*"I've been told the best singles bars
are meat markets."*

4

DATING

or
This Could Be the
Start of
Something Big

Before I left Russia, I had many fears about moving to the United States. And I think that no matter what country you're coming from, the fears are pretty much the same. Some of you may be worried about how quickly you'll be able to pick up the language. In my particular case, I was worried about how quickly I'd be able to pick up a girl.

Fortunately I read an article in *Cosmopolitan* that a friend of mine had smuggled in; it really put my mind at ease. The article said, "In America, sex is for the asking." So when I arrived in New York, I had a million questions.

Okay, guys, now it's time for some straight talk about when you go out on that first date. There's something that you must have with you. It's more important than your car keys. It's even more important than your wallet. And yes, it's for your own personal protection. I'm talking about a . . . dictionary! That's right, a dictionary, because language differences can create a lot of problems on a date. If you take a dictionary, maybe you can avoid some of the embarrassing moments I've had. For instance, just like in French, the Russian word for "shower" is *douche*. On my first date in America, I told the girl that I was so nervous about going out, I spent an hour douching. I never saw *her* again.

Another American word that confused me was "yep." "Yep" in English means "yes," but in Russian it means "sex." This is true, I'm not making it up. When I arrived in the U.S., all I heard was everyone saying "yep, yep, yep, yep, yep." I thought to myself, "What a country!"

I even met a girl who said she was part of the Yuppie Movement. Well, I thought she said "Yeppie," and I figured the more movement, the better.

Once I asked a friend of mine, "Would you like to do something tonight?" He said, "Yep." I said, "Nope!"

Now, that was one of the big surprises to me about America. You see, we don't have gay people in the Soviet Union. We have homosexuals, they're just not allowed to be gay about it. Actually, homosexuality is a crime, and the punishment is seven years in prison, locked up with other men—and there is a three-year waiting list for that.

Now don't get me wrong. Sex in Russia is a lot of fun as long as you follow the rules. For instance, no one is allowed to have a second orgasm until everyone else in the country has had one.

When you first arrive in the USA, you should expect to undergo a short period of adjustment to your new country. This is completely normal. It may take you a while to learn to like some things, such as the food and clothing. Some other things may take a little longer for you to learn to like because they're more of an acquired taste, such as the music and literature. And there are going to be still other things that, no matter how long you try, you'll always find irritating and never learn to like . . . such as Barry Manilow. But the one thing that you will definitely enjoy immediately in the United States is the women. They're so different here. American women are free! Well, a few of them charge, but most of them are free. . . . I'm just kidding. Most of them charge. Yep!

Women in the Soviet Union are much different. As a matter of fact, Russian men have a saying: "Women are like buses . . ." That's it. I'm just kidding. I don't want to make fun of Russian women, because some of them may be reading this book, and they'll kick my ass.

Actually, I sympathize with Russian women, because there aren't many products made for them. For example, they don't have Oil of Olay. They get Lard of Olay. Perfumes are sold under names like An Evening in Prison. Or Chernobyl No. 5. And the only birth-control device available to women is the sponge—an S.O.S. pad. (It's a heavy metal sound.) As you can see, it's not easy being a Russian woman.

Now, no matter what country you've come from, you're probably familiar with those infamous institutions that specialize in torture and pain: singles bars. They have them here in the United States and they have them in the Soviet Union. But trust me on this: the American ones are much better. When you go to a Russian singles bar, you "get lucky" if you go home alone. I quickly learned that I couldn't use any of my old standard pickup lines here; the ones that had worked so well in the USSR. Lines like "Can I buy you a potato?" and "Would you like to come back to my place for a nightmare?" My own personal favorite was "Would you like to defect?" It never failed. One night I defected six times. Yep! Once in an American singles bar, a real sexy girl asked me, "What sign are you?"

I said, "I'm a Leo." Actually, I was born in January, but in Russia the government tells you what your sign will be. If they have a shortage of Leos, you're a Leo.

Unfortunately, if you want to meet women in the United States, you almost have to go to bars. If singles bars aren't your cup of tea, it's still possible to meet women, but you've got to be clever and resourceful. You can learn from some of my experiences, because I have tried everything. I heard that one great way to meet women was to join an organization and get involved in some of its activities. Looking back, I suppose I could have made a better choice than the YMCA . . . but at least I learned how to swim.

I made another attempt by placing an ad in the personals column. I said that I was tall, dark, and handsome and I got an immediate response—the Better Business Bureau charged me with false advertising.

Out of sheer desperation, I asked a friend of mine how he got dates, and he told me that he met a lot of women when he did his laundry. That sounded like a pretty good idea, so I did *his* laundry. But I didn't meet any girls. In fact, the only person I met was the Maytag repairman . . . and he said he wasn't that lonely. My friend must have felt some pity for me, because the next night he said he was going to take me to the ultimate "meat market." I told him that I really didn't need any meat, but I wouldn't mind picking up a few vegetables. And he said, "Don't worry, we probably will."

Depending on how desperate you get for a woman, there is always that one final alternative, a blind date. I found out that Americans don't particularly like blind dates because you don't get to see the girl first. (In Russia, that was the best part!) While they may not be too popular in the United States, they can be educational. Thanks to a blind date here, I learned the English translation for the word "ugly." It means "nice personality." As a matter of fact, that blind date reminded me of my first Russian girlfriend, Olga Turnyorheadandkov. She had a face that could stop the spread of communism! I only went out with her because she had a reputation as the type of girl who can't say *nyet.*

Olga had quite a crush on me. And "crush" is the perfect word for it, because when a Russian woman jumps your bones, she breaks them. The funny thing is, though, I never knew she wasn't beautiful until I came to America and saw what other women look like. I mean, if you've never seen anything better than what you have, you don't know what you're missing. It's kind of like people who live in Cleveland. And I don't want to offend Cleveland, because I really like that city. It has, well, a nice personality.

Dating in the United States may not be all that different from dating in your native country. For example, on a typical American date, a couple might go to dinner and a movie. On a typical Russian date, a couple might go to a movie about people eating dinner. And if there's one thing that proves all men in the world are really the same, it's got to be sitting in a dark movie theater with a girl. We're all waiting and hoping for the same thing . . . to "cop a feel." (Now, that's an interesting American expression. Originally I thought it was "feel a cop," but that's a story I'd rather not go into.) With the theater lights low, and the movie on, I'd try to, as you Americans say, "grab a little tit." But in Russia, there's no such thing as a "little tit." It would be lying all over your lap. I'd be saying, "Get that thing off of me! And come down from the balcony!"

By now you're probably wondering what you can expect from an American woman on a date. Well, the only thing that you can truly expect is the unexpected. Let me give you an illustration of this by telling you about my last three dates. The first one I met when I enrolled in a health club. (By the way, if you also decide to join one, be sure to get yourself a good pair of running shoes. A friend of mine told me that Nikes are a very good brand. Unfortunately, I thought he said Knockers, so I went to a store and asked the girl, "Do you have Knockers?" She answered, "What, are you blind?" I replied, "No, I want to try them on for size." She said, "They're going to be too big for you." It ended up costing me fifty dollars . . . and they weren't that big.) Anyway, the main reason I joined a health club was that after living in the Soviet Union for twenty-six years, I was already pretty good at running. I met a female body builder there and asked her out. I picked her up at seven. She picked *me* up at eight, nine, and ten. It was embarrassing. I was going to spend the night at her place until I saw the sign hanging over her bed: NO PAIN, NO GAIN. I got out of there in a hurry.

The second date was when a girl invited me over to her house for dinner. I was pretty excited and really looking forward to it, until she called and asked me to bring over some California wine, Philadelphia Cream Cheese, and Maine lobster. By the time I got back from all those places, she was married . . . but at least I added eight thousand miles to my frequent-flyer program.

My third date was very special. It was with a woman from California, one of those Valley Girls. They talk so funny, saying things like "fer sure" and "bitchin." I asked this Valley Girl if she'd like to go back to my apartment, and she said, "Hey man, I'm not buying it."

I told her, "Neither am I, I'm renting it."

Then she said, "Oh gag me" . . . so I did.

She was kind of young, about nineteen, so the next morning

I was feeling a little guilty and I said to her, "Tell me the truth, was I the first?"

She turned to me and said, "You could have been, your face looks familiar."

I said, "Oh gag me!"

I guess if there's one thing I've learned since coming to this country, it's how similar we all are. Russian men want the same things out of life as American men . . . American women! Yep!

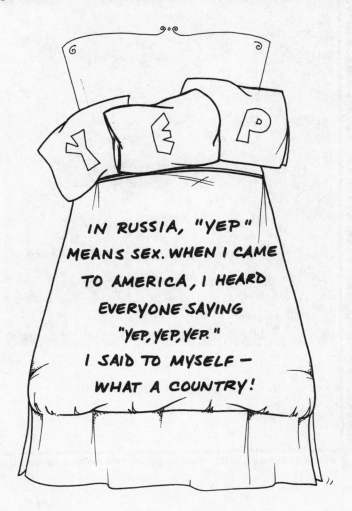

IN RUSSIA, "YEP"
MEANS SEX. WHEN I CAME
TO AMERICA, I HEARD
EVERYONE SAYING
"YEP, YEP, YEP."
I SAID TO MYSELF —
WHAT A COUNTRY!

"Learning pigeon English can be messy."

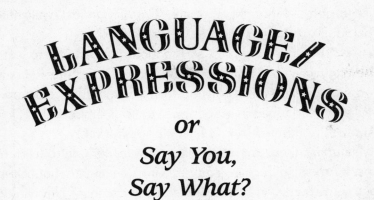

5

LANGUAGE/ EXPRESSIONS

or
Say You,
Say What?

The secret to survival in the United States is twofold. First, when at the airport, you must never strike up a conversation with a bald man wearing a sheet and selling flowers. And second, you must learn the language. Now, learning to speak English is easy. But learning to speak English like an *American* is the hard part. Americans have a very colorful language. There are many different meanings of the same word or phrase. I will be giving you several examples later in this chapter, but first let me teach you two of the most important and useful phrases that you will ever need to know.

The first is "But Officer, she said she was eighteen!" Hopefully, you won't need to use that one too often.

The other phrase will come in handy when nature calls. The correct way to ask is "Where may I go to the bathroom?" With any luck the response you get will be "The facilities are right over there." Be prepared for any response, though. The first time I asked that question, I was told, "Go down the hall and use the john." I thought to myself, "Boy, John must really hate that job!"

Now, I was in a big rush, so I thought the best way to learn the language would be through television. I locked myself in my room and watched TV nonstop for three months . . . before I realized I had tuned in a Spanish station. (I suppose that Desi Arnaz Film Festival should have tipped me off.)

Naturally, there are many different ways for you to learn to speak American English. You can enroll in a night-school class, buy some books and tapes and study at home, or you can do what I finally did and just learn from being around Americans. Translation dictionaries are helpful, but I learned more accurate definitions of words and phrases through my everyday dealings with people in the United States than I ever could have learned from a book. If you do it my way, then the whole country becomes your school, and everyone you meet will be your teacher. In fact, the first teacher I had was a used-car salesman. He taught me the meaning of the phrase "trust me." It means "bend over." Like all foreigners, when you first start to learn the language, you will begin by speaking pigeon English. You won't mind, because old ladies will feed you bread crumbs. (The really hard part is learning how to crap on windshields.)

Many things that may confuse you are simply the expressions you will regularly encounter in your everyday life. I recently had just such an experience in a restaurant. I was about to order dessert, and the waitress suggested I try the cheesecake.

I told her, "I don't like cheesecake, do you have any Jell-O?"

She said, "Yes, I have plenty of Jell-O. I have Jell-O coming out of my ears!"

I said, "I'll have cheesecake."

Some Americans will mix you up unintentionally, even when they're trying to help you. A friend of mine once tried to give me a tip so I could get into the stock market. He said, "I got it straight from the horse's mouth." Now, I'm thinking to myself, "There's a great source of information." When I hesitated, he said, "Maybe you'll find it hard to swallow." I replied, "If you got it from the horse's mouth, I don't even want to touch it!" Then he told me that if I didn't take his advice, I'd end up "paying through the nose." I said, "I'll have cheesecake."

Honestly, it can be enough to drive a man to drink. But even if you're in a bar, you're not safe from these crazy phrases. The first time I visited one, I heard the bartender say, "The drinks are on the house." I turned to the guy next to me and asked him what that meant.

"It means the drinks are free."

I thought to myself, "Big deal, if you've got to climb on the roof to get them."

There are certain phrases you'll hear all the time, like "hang in there," "hang tough," and "hang around." After hearing these expressions so many times, I asked a friend of mine if it was important to be "hung" in America. He said, "It certainly is popular with the girls."

The way Americans speak can be different depending on what part of the country you are in. For example, you'll notice that down south the people are constantly checking your hearing. They are always saying things like "Drive careful, ya hear?" and "You come back now, ya hear?" Apparently they have some eye problems down there too. Once I went by myself to a restaurant in North Carolina and the waitress said, "You all come on in." I looked around to see if there was someone else standing there. There was no one. Then she seated me. "What would you all like to order?" she asked, and later, she said, "You all come back now." I said, "We all didn't even leave yet, ya hear?"

I don't think that the average American realizes how easily things like that confuse us. I was appearing in a nightclub in Texas last year, and after my performance, the owner came up to me and said, "You know, you're getting a little hoarse." I said, "Well, I usually get paid in cash, but I'll take a horse."

Texans have a very strange sense of humor. This club owner took me to his ranch and played a practical joke on me . . . he had me milk his bull. Let me tell you something: you milk this animal once, you've got a friend for life. That bull was following me around all weekend going, "You all come back now, ya hear?"

Being in show business, I guess I have more strangers come up to talk with me than someone might have in another line of work. And I've heard so many crazy expressions that I could probably write a book. (Oh yeah, I *am* writing a book.) After my performance at The Comedy Store in Los Angeles, a girl came up to me and said, "I enjoyed your show. I had a gas." Now, I appreciated the honesty, but I didn't need to know about her personal problem.

Some of the most difficult things for me to learn were show-business expressions. After I had performed for my first American audience, another comedian came up to me backstage and said, "Man, you really killed them!" I hid from the police for a month, thinking what a dangerous business comedy must be here. And I can't tell you how many times I've had someone come up to me and say, "My mother-in-law would die for your autograph." Since I've become famous, my pen has turned into a deadly weapon.

We all learn at our own pace, and some people pick up the

language quicker than others. Of course, if you have an incentive, that helps. My mom learned English very quickly because she had a big goal . . . to be able to nag me in two languages. (Just kidding, Mom.) Actually, my parents, like a lot of people who have come to the United States later in life, have had some problems learning to understand and speak English. The first American phrase they learned was "What's on sale?" Unfortunately, the second phrase they learned was "Charge it!" Somehow they never learned how to say "Just looking."

Confusing expressions can be doubly frustrating for older people because they tend to take things so much more seriously. When they heard the TV commercial that said, "Please don't squeeze the Charmin," they thought it must be against the law. And then there was the time a few years ago when I was doing a television show for Dick Clark Productions and the producers decided that they'd like to film an interview with my parents. Normally they would have said no because they're kind of shy, but this time they agreed to do it. (They like Dick Clark because he's older than they are.) The director called them up and said, "We'll be out to shoot you on Thursday." I got home and my parents were scared. They said, "Why do they want to shoot us? We didn't squeeze the Charmin!" I told them I was sure it was just a misunderstanding, but to be on the safe side we left town for two weeks. I mean, you never know . . . ABC? . . . KGB? . . .

If there was one piece of advice I could give you above all others in this chapter, it would be "Don't be ashamed if you do something wrong." I misunderstood so many things when I first came to the United States that I made more bad decisions than Richard Nixon. Every time I turned around it seemed like I was embarrassing myself—and it really wasn't my fault. I mean, when the garbage collector came to my house, I was told to give him all my garbage. So when the bill collector came to my house . . . I gave him all my bills. Well, I'll tell you something, the garbage man was a lot more grateful.

At this point, I think it would be useful if I were to give you a few common American expressions and then tell you what they really mean. Here are some samples:

1. *"The check is in the mail"* means, depending on the spelling, either that someone hasn't sent out your money yet, or a gay guy from Czechoslovakia got lucky on a date.

2. *"Think of it as an investment"* means "Think of it as overpriced."

3. *"Of course it's tax deductible"* means "Welcome to prison."

4. *"The shit hit the fan"* means "Uh-oh."

5. *"You can earn up to a thousand dollars a day"* means "Forget it! It's either illegal or it's Herbalife."

Well, hopefully I've given you some help in deciphering the American language. With a little hard work, you should soon be able to read, write, and speak English. Once you have that mastered, you can tackle a truly impossible task: learning how to program your VCR!

WE HAVE A SAYING IN RUSSIA: "WOMEN ARE LIKE BUSES . . ." THAT'S IT.

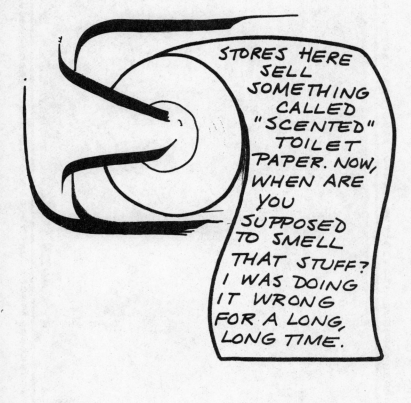

"Yuck! In Russia, we don't eat this
part of the dog."

6

FOOD

or
Looking for Lox
in All the
Wrong Places

The day I arrived in the United States, I had my first real American breakfast—English muffins, French toast, and Canadian bacon. After that meal, I fell in love with the food in the USA, and you will too.

The best way to experience American food is just to dig right in. Depending on what country you're coming from, it may seem different to you at first. It's certainly different from food in the Soviet Union. And the main difference is that here you have it. I don't want to give you the impression that Russians don't have as much to eat as Americans, because that's not true. It's just that we take a little more time between meals—like a weekend!

Most all new immigrants arriving in the United States bring stories of how terrible the food situation was in their native country. In Russia the food situation was also pretty bad, but never so terrible that my mother would put an empty plate in front of me and say, "Starve, there are children eating in America."

And yet I do seem to remember a nursery rhyme she'd read to me at dinnertime that went, "Old Mother Hubbard went to the cupboard to get her poor dog." (Okay, that sounds pretty gross. That is, until you see an American eating a hot dog. In Russia, we don't eat that part of the dog.) In fairness to Americans, they're not the only ones who eat disgusting things. Take the people who live in France, for example. They have to make meals out of snails and frog's legs. Considering what they're forced to eat, it's no wonder French waiters are so rude.

In my particular case, I think I would have welcomed snails and frog's legs compared to what I had to eat in the Soviet Union. My mother did the best she could to feed me. She would give me hard black bread and a potato that she'd plucked right out of the ground and say, "Eat, it's good for you." I became a vegetarian, but not by choice.

The reason there is a food shortage in the first place is that the government stockpiles all the food for the Russian army. Now, whatever the army doesn't use after a year, the government sells to the public. Of course, by then it's very stale and very expensive . . . kind of like food at 7-Eleven. When food finally does become available, you have to stand in long lines to buy it. In fact, you have to stand in long lines for everything in the Soviet Union. Sometimes, if you are very lucky, you might get into an express line—ten miles or less.

Because the lines in Russia are so long, sometimes you can't always see what they're selling. You might think that you are in line for toilet paper, and then seven hours later you'll get to the front and discover they're selling chickens. But after standing there for seven hours, chicken will do . . . it's soft, warm, and you can squeeze it! The line that I hated the most was for Wonder Bread. I'd stand in line and wonder if I was going to get bread. Whenever I'd get the chance, I'd buy one loaf of white bread and one loaf of black bread. The difference between them was two years.

One of the most popular Soviet meals is the bread sandwich. That is two slices of bread with another slice of bread in between. For those of you who might like to sample one, they have the same thing in America—it's called a Big Mac. It's okay, but there's still nothing like real Russian bread made from real Kansas wheat.

Even when there was a lot of food, it was often difficult keeping it fresh. When I was a kid, most people couldn't afford a refrigerator. To keep the food cold, we would hang it out the window. The government used to brag that every kitchen in Moscow came equipped with an automatic defroster—it's called summer.

As you've probably already discovered, there are no such problems in the United States. Food is plentiful here, and there is a variety of supermarkets and restaurants to choose from. For those of you on a limited budget, there are many bargains to be found, particularly in restaurants. One of the best is the all-you-can-eat buffet. Restaurants in the Soviet Union also have them. There they give you a piece of bread and say, "That's all you can eat." Of course, that really simplifies etiquette: "What wine goes with nothing?"

As bad as it was trying to get something to eat at home in the USSR, it was even worse in the restaurants. Whenever I went to a Russian restaurant, I would always have reservations—but I would go anyway. And you knew what kind of a dining experience you were in for because the sign in the window would say, SORRY, WE'RE OPEN. For those of you who think it costs a lot to eat in an American restaurant, you should try doing it in the Soviet Union. Restaurant food in Russia is so expensive that it's like having to choose between ordering a chicken and a car . . . and you usually order the chicken because they offer 8.8 percent financing!

Because there are so many restaurants in the United States, you'll have to learn to be selective. The very first American restaurant I visited was Denny's. We didn't have Denny's in Russia—thank God! What a strange place. When I went in to be seated, the hostess asked me, "How many in your party?" I said, "Two million." She gave me a corner booth.

You may start to wonder about some of the people who work there. They all seem to look the same. I was curious to know if, to hire someone there, they require a three-pimple minimum. The hardest thing to get used to is the service they give. I ordered a hamburger in one place and the waiter asked me if I wanted him to "hold my pickle." I said, "No thanks, not while I'm eating. I've been doing it myself for years, and I'm pretty happy about it." Then he asked if he could "toast my buns." When he offered me some "secret sauce," I decided to take my meal "to go." When he said he was going to put it in a doggie bag, I just stuffed the food in my pockets and left.

Some waiters may try to take advantage of you if they think you're a foreigner. Fortunately, I've become a pretty sophisticated diner and they can't put anything over on me. For instance, the other night a waitress wanted to bring me the chef's salad . . . but I made her get me one of my own. You've got to be sharp. Let me give you a couple of tips from my own experience. If someone offers you a finger sandwich, say yes. If someone offers you a knuckle sandwich, say no. Just trust me on that one.

You've also got to be careful because some restaurants will

just plain lie to you. I remember one very embarrassing moment I had. Have you seen the McDonald's commercials where they claim "We do it all for you"? Well, don't believe it, because it's not true. I went to McDonald's and the girl at the counter refused to do it all for me. In fact, she refused to do any of it for me. I had to go to Burger King to get it "my way."

Another problem I had was at the drive-thru window. Who are they kidding? There's no way that I could drive through that little thing. And after they take your order they tell you to drive around. I drove around for twenty minutes. I got dizzy, and my food got cold.

Since dining out can be complicated, you might decide to start having more of your meals at home. That's what I did. I was eating a lot of frozen dinners when I realized that they would probably taste better if they were warm. (I really hate crunchy gravy.) So I bought a used microwave oven at a garage sale for twenty-five dollars. The only problem was that it didn't have a door. After using it for a month, I decided to buy a door . . . and eventually my eyebrows grew back. I'm okay now, but my cat gave birth to a guppy. I realize that I didn't get a very good buy, but you've got to understand that in Russia we never had anything like a microwave oven. They do now, though . . . it's called Chernobyl. (By the way, do you know how to make chicken Kiev? First you preheat the city to four hundred degrees . . .)

Once you begin to understand American food, you'll want to start eating things that are good for you. If you really want to learn which foods will help you live the longest, you may want to do what I did and consult a nutritionist. I went to a very famous one in Hollywood. He had worked for Orson Welles. After running dozens of tests and charging me $1,100, he gave me his recommendations. He suggested that I eat hard black bread and potatoes plucked right from the ground . . . and take some more time between meals—like a weekend.

"As a matter of fact," he said, "do you know what country eats really healthy?" I said, "I know! I know!"

"Joan who?"

7

TELEVISION/ MOVIES

or
We've Only
Just Rerun

In the language chapter, I left out one phrase that is crucial if you are going to live in the United States. It's those three little words that are dearest to every American's heart: "What's on TV?"

Television, also known as the "boob tube" (which is why I thought everybody had two) or the "idiot box" (which I figured out after I saw "The Newlywed Game") is truly America's national pastime. It will influence every part of your life here. I asked a girl out once and she said, "First, I have to ask you three questions: Have you got a wife? Have you got any communicable diseases? Have you got cable?" (Fortunately, I knew what cable was because I'd had it in Russia—it just wasn't attached to a TV. It just lay on the floor, so when friends came over, you could point to it and say, "I got cable.")

At first I got depressed watching American television because it made me realize how bad my English was. I watched a lot of cartoons and even Scooby-Doo spoke better than I did!

But then one night I watched a Sylvester Stallone movie, and suddenly I felt much better. Gradually, you learn to enjoy and appreciate your TV, but you will probably have a lot of the same questions I did, such as: "If 'Fantasy Island' really works, then why isn't 'Tattoo' six foot three?" And what the hell is "ring around the collar" anyway? But television can teach you a lot about yourself. For instance, I had no idea how badly I wanted my MTV until David Bowie started telling me three hundred times a day!

What will probably amaze you most about American television is the variety of programming there is to choose from. I don't know about your country, but in Russia we only had two channels: Channel one was propaganda. On channel two, there was a KGB officer telling you, "Turn back to channel one!"

Americans sometimes criticize their TV shows for being unoriginal, but that's because they haven't seen what television is like in other parts of the world. For example, I now know that the shows we had in Russia were just remakes of American TV series. We had to watch comedies like "Marx and Mindy," "Unhappy Days," and "Leave It to Brezhnev." Soviet soap operas had titles like "One Day to Live" and "Search for All My Children." If you didn't like the soaps, your only other choice was game shows such as "Bowling for Food" and "Wheel of Torture." But I'll tell you, my favorite show was the one about the guy who has the chance to leave Russia, but doesn't. It was called "That's Incredible!" And "Wonder Woman" . . . she looks like a woman, but you wonder.

If you have children, you'll appreciate the educational programming on American TV. The only educational show I saw as a child was "Comrade Rogers" ("Can you say 'Siberia'?"). And for you people who love talk shows, America is definitely the late-night place to be. Russian TV is famous for their "don't talk" shows such as "Shut Your Face!" But at least there was no Richard Simmons.

Thanks to satellite dishes and recent developments in American technology, many of you will still be able to see some television programming from your homeland. I was surprised to see the changes made in Soviet TV since I left. Russians now have their own pay movie channel—CineMarx. The other night I watched *Commie Dearest*. (I'll never forget that scene with the barbed-wire coat hangers.) And Mikhail Gorbachev is producing a new series to help find future Russian leaders; it's called "Czar Search."

While living here, you'll find television a great source for news. Unlike the tightly controlled media in other countries, American journalists have the freedom to tackle any subject matter they want. From female mud wrestlers to bottomless bikinis, American TV reporters uncover it all. And the news programs here are obviously far superior to any I saw in Russia. There they had programs like "Issues and No Answers" and "Face the Firing Squad." And in America, you can see the news as it happens. In Russia, the news was always on a slight delay . . . like a few years. I recently received a call from a friend in Russia who told me he was "sorry to hear about the *Titanic*"! Soviet news shows also tend to be a little bit slanted, such as the day anchorman Dan Rathernot came on and announced, "Peace-seeking missile struck by Korean airliner! No film at eleven."

Of course, American news programs also have a strange way of reporting events. They have a tendency to look on the negative side. For instance, if a plane crashes but no one dies, rather than report "All one hundred people survived," they will tell you "One hundred people *could* have been killed." And they don't stop there. They'll add on details like, "If the plane had crashed only two blocks to the west, it would have hit a nursing home—which is only three miles from a children's playground." Now, if this plane had crashed in Russia, the story would have been handled very differently. They would have just built an airport around it and said, "The plane just landed early!"

I would not be doing my job unless I informed you about the absolute worst part of American television. It's called a commercial and no matter how hard you try, there is no way to escape one. I strongly suggest you do not watch your first commercial alone. There is no telling what you might see. It could be a dancing cat. Or singing raisins. Or a man driving a motorboat inside a toilet. And then they'll tell you, don't use drugs!

Commercials on American television sometimes pop up in very ironic places. The other night I watched a movie about the bombing of Pearl Harbor, sponsored by Toyota! The ad said, "You asked for it, you got it!"

American products also like to challenge each other on TV. A Russian advertising agency tried to do one of those "taste test" commercials, but they couldn't get anyone to put on the blindfold.

Here is a sample script from a Soviet commercial:

> SOLDIER #1: Want to invade any more countries?
> SOLDIER #2: Nah.
> SOLDIER #1: How about for a Michelob Light?
> SOLDIER #2: Start the tanks!

For me to say that all American commercials are annoying, insulting, and an irritating waste of intelligent viewers' time would really be unfair and untrue. I'm kind of fond of those Lite Beer ads. . . .

"I like to get as much freedom as possible."

SHOPPING/ PRODUCTS

or
How Much Is
That Ferrari
in the Window?

Coming from the Soviet Union, I was not prepared for the incredible variety of products available in American grocery stores. I couldn't believe all the wonderful things they have. On my first shopping trip, I saw powdered milk . . . you just add water, and you get milk. Then I saw powdered orange juice . . . you just add water, and you get orange juice. And then I saw baby powder. . . . I thought to myself, "What a country!" I'm making my family tonight!

The first thing that you will probably notice about the grocery stores in America is how very generous they are. Everywhere you look there are boxes and cans of food that say "Try this!" or "Try some!" I don't know about you, but I get so stuffed on my shopping trips that I usually don't have to buy anything.

One aisle that you should particularly enjoy is the cereal aisle. Many of the boxes there tell you things like "Look Inside for Free Surprise!" What a country! Of course, you'll have to dump all that cereal onto the floor to find it.

There are so many wonderful items in American stores. But you've got to be careful about what you purchase. Some products here don't have very good directions on how to use them. For instance, in many stores you will see something for sale called "scented toilet paper." Now, unfortunately, it doesn't tell you *when* you're supposed to smell that stuff. I was doing it wrong for a long, long time.

After a lifetime of shopping in the USSR, there were a lot of adjustments I had to make when I visited a store here. In the beginning, I had a great deal of trouble getting used to American shopping carts. You see, in Russia, they're armed with surface-to-air missiles. (You may not be able to put as many groceries in them, but nobody will cut in line ahead of you either.)

Depending on what country you've come from, you're bound to see some products that you aren't familiar with. For example, in the dairy section there are two things that are just mind-boggling. First, they have these containers that hold a dozen eggs. You'll probably have the same question I had: how do they get twelve chickens to sit so close together? And if that isn't amazing enough, they also sell sour cream in these tiny little containers. I figure American cows must have incredible aim!

Now, with all these new products to learn about, even I made a few errors at first. I remember buying Kitty Litter because I thought it was cheap cereal. I mean, it tasted like grape nuts. Several months later, someone told me what it really was. Since that day, I get nervous whenever a cat gets a little too close.

Some products will seem strange to you. When I saw Perrier water selling for a dollar a bottle, I thought it was a joke. Until

I tasted it . . . and then I *knew* it was a joke. Then there are items they sell with confusing names like Love My Carpet. Now, I can only speak for myself here, but at best I might *like* my carpet. Anything more intimate would not only be sick, but could also cause rug burns.

You see, in the Soviet Union we didn't have things like that. In fact, there were even some American products that were banned in the USSR. The government made it illegal for Russian stores to sell Visine because "it gets the red out."

There are some similar items sold in both countries, though, like soft drinks. The main difference is that in the United States there are many different brands, and in the Soviet Union there are only two: Commie Cola and Pop-aganda. The Russians also have their version of Lite Beer: "everything you always wanted in a beer . . . or else!"

The nice thing about shopping in supermarkets in America is that it's really a lot of fun. If you're feeling a little run-down, you can go to the health section and find a hundred different brands of vitamins. Personally I recommend the Flintstones vitamins. I don't know if they're really that much better than the others, but I always seem to get a lift after eating Wilma (although I do feel a little funny swallowing Barney).

You'll find each aisle has a new adventure waiting for you. I've only had one unpleasant experience in an American grocery store, and that was on my first shopping trip. I accidentally walked down one aisle and found dog food. At first this threw me, because in Russia, dogs *are* food. I found myself staring at cans that had pictures of dogs and cats on them, and I said to myself, "Ugh. Not this stuff again." Some of them even had little poodles and chihuahuas on them. Who eats that stuff? I guess when Americans say that they're going to get some chow for lunch, they're not kidding.

There is one marvelous product, though, that men may want to check out. It's a new kind of baby bottle they claim is "as good as natural breast-feeding." When I saw that, I said to myself, "What a country!" I bought two of them! They're great, and the best part is—no personal commitment.

Supermarkets aren't the only stores you can shop in. To get some idea of what kind of stores are out there waiting for you, all you have to do is pick up a newspaper and look at the ads. I should warn you that some ads are very misleading. For example, I recently read an ad in the paper that said, "Big Sale, Last Week!" Now, if the sale was "last week," then why advertise? I've already missed it, they're just rubbing it in.

And you've got to be careful about some of the claims these companies make in their ads. There is another store in town that says, "We Guarantee Our Furniture and Stand Behind It for Six Months!" I don't want people standing behind my furniture. That's why I left the Soviet Union.

The hardest thing for me to learn was how to shop for clothes. There are so many stores here and so many different brands and designers. It was much simpler in the USSR. Most of the clothing there is made in Poland . . . and they tell you, "Don't look for the union label." Actually, there were a few Russian designer brand names like Calvin Kremlin and Comrade Klein. The biggest was Party Members Only.

Now, if you've come from a Communist country, as I have, the thing you probably appreciate most about American clothing stores is how easy it is to get blue jeans. In Russia, American blue jeans are very scarce, so they're pretty expensive. You can only buy them on the black market, and they normally cost about 500 dollars a pair. That's because the Americans are usually still in them. That's why most Russians have the "501 Blues"—because they can't get any.

In general, though, you'll enjoy shopping in clothing stores here in the U.S. But let me warn you that some salesmen have a weird sense of humor. In particular, watch out for shoe salesmen, because they think they're the funniest. Recently, I went in for a pair of shoes and asked a salesman what he had in my size. He suggested wing tips. Now, I know I've got large feet, but . . . (Anyway, I outsmarted him. I bought some shoe trees, and as soon as they start to blossom I won't have to worry about spending money on Florsheims anymore.)

The best way for you to learn how to be a good shopper is to just go out and buy things. Go out and buy a car! Go out and buy a house! Go out and buy another copy of this book! Even though I'm now a pretty sophisticated shopper, I'm still sometimes overwhelmed by the amazing freedom of choice we have in stores. For instance, I was recently in a supermarket and I saw something called New Freedom. Freedom in a box! I said to myself, "What a country!" I bought fifteen of them, with wings and everything. I got "super-maxi" because I wanted as much freedom as possible. Nobody would tell me what those things were for. At first, I thought they were napkins . . . so I put them on the dining room table. Then I began to notice that people weren't hanging around for dessert anymore. Then I thought they were headbands. I wore one when I went to the health club to work out. It was the first time I ever had the showers all to myself. Finally I started sending them to my friends in Russia, so they could have some freedom too. Of course, since then I've gotten quite a bit smarter. Now I only buy Stayfree.

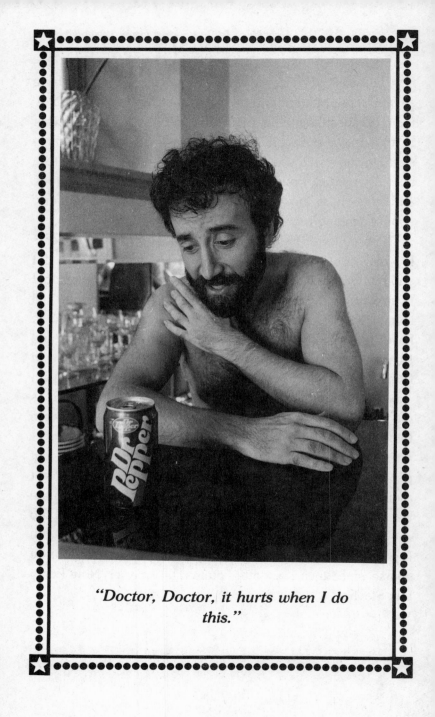

"Doctor, Doctor, it hurts when I do this."

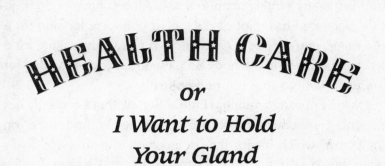

9

HEALTH CARE
or
I Want to Hold Your Gland

In the Soviet Union, health care is free . . . and you get what you pay for.

Doctors in the USSR are a lot different from American physicians. For example, if you go to a Russian doctor for a checkup, he won't waste a lot of time and money on preliminary tests—he'll go straight to the autopsy. Now, I don't want to give you the impression that the Soviet government is against modern medical advances. Actually, Russia was one of the first countries in the world to develop nuclear medicine—they put a rubber glove on a missile and told Afghanistan to bend over!

It is also the only nation in the world to have a machine that gives everyone in the country X rays at the same time . . . it's called Chernobyl.

Choosing your doctor is probably the second most important decision you will ever have to make in the United States. (The first is whether Lite Beer tastes great or is less filling.) Finding a doctor sounds a lot more complicated than it really is. It just takes a little common sense. All you have to do is go to a place that has a lot of doctors. If you were looking for a mechanic, you'd go to a gas station. If you were looking for a teacher, you'd go to a school. So naturally, if you're looking for a doctor, you go to a . . . golf course!

Maybe I'm exaggerating a little. After all, that's certainly not the only place you'll find doctors. You may also find some "on the court," which means they're involved in tennis, and that's okay; but if you find one *in* the court, that means they're involved in malpractice and you should return to the golf course immediately!

Now, when I started looking for a physician, I figured that the best one would be whoever advertised the most on television . . . Dr. Pepper. But he was not an *easy* guy to find. I'd call hospitals and ask for Dr. Pepper and they'd hang up on me. Finally I asked a friend where I could find him and he said, "You'll find Dr. Pepper in a bottle." And I thought to myself, "Another career shattered by drinking."

Once you find a doctor you can go in for a checkup. Now, be prepared to be asked a lot of questions by the nurse before you ever see the doctor. The first thing she said to me was that she needed my history. I told her that first there was Khrushchev, then Brezhnev, and now Gorbachev.

She said, "No, I mean, what has made you sick?"

I said, "Khrushchev, Brezhnev, and Gorbachev."

Finally she just came out and asked me if, for example, I'd had chicken pox.

I told her, "No, but I've had Chicken McNuggets."

She said, "Chicken pox are better for you."

Finally, after you get through all the questions, it's time to see the doctor. Now, this is where choosing the right doctor is so important. There are many different kinds of physicians in the United States, and many are specialists. And some of their specialties are a little strange. I ended up with just such a doctor. He told me he was an "ear, nose, and throat man." Personally, I'm a "leg man" myself, but I figure whatever turns you on. He examined me and said he'd like to take my tonsils out. I thought to myself, "That's weird. Can't he get a girl like everybody else?"

Some of these doctors write books that Americans buy. And a lot of these books are about sex. A friend of mine suggested that I buy one that was written by Dr. Ruth. I went to the bookstore and got the name a little mixed up and ended up buying a book by Dr. Seuss. It was great, but for a while, instead of getting turned on by a girl in a skirt, I started having fantasies about a cat in a hat.

Finally I found myself a normal doctor, and he gave me a complete examination. You should be aware of what a complete examination in America covers. It includes a blood-pressure check, a heartbeat check, and a credit check. (Not necessarily in that order.) Hopefully everything will be all right with you. In my case, the doctor found a problem. He told me, "You have mono and hemorrhoids . . . so you can kiss your ass good-bye!"

He wanted me to go to the hospital. Going to a hospital in any country can be a little frightening, even here in the United States. First off, the names of the hospitals I've seen don't exactly inspire confidence. I had a choice of going to Smith *Memorial* Hospital or Johnson *Memorial* Hospital. Now, if they couldn't save Smith or Johnson, what chance did I have?

Another thing that may scare you is the terminology they use in the hospital. I was in there waiting to be admitted when they wheeled in a guy who had been shot in the head, and the doctor said he was in "satisfactory condition." I'm thinking to myself, "There's a guy who's easy to please!"

The only pleasant experiences you may have in a hospital will be the nurses. I had a wonderful nurse on my floor . . . actually, I had her twice. Many nurses are also specialists. I met a surgical nurse and a maternity nurse, but I never did get to meet the one that interested me the most . . . the head nurse.

One thing that surprised me and may also surprise you is that most nurses are registered nurses. Isn't that ridiculous? They register nurses, but they don't register guns! I figured that nurses must be more dangerous than guns. One night I was sitting in a bar when a guy walked in with a loaded nurse—I hit the floor!

No chapter on health care would be complete unless it covered dentists. There are two unpleasant experiences in life that are unavoidable. One is seeing a dentist, the other is seeing an episode of "Gilligan's Island." In Russia, dentistry is performed without any frills. Soviet dentists never use Novocain. So that they won't waste all that pain, the KGB asks you questions while they're drilling. A typical conversation in a Russian dentist's chair might go something like this: "Rinse. Spit. Where were you on the night of August 23?" It's a pretty good incentive to brush after every meal.

American dentists are much more advanced. First off, they use gold or silver to fill your cavities. In Russia, they use lead . . . from forty feet away.

You will really love dentists in the United States. What I liked best was that gas they give you so you don't feel anything. I love that stuff. My first month in America, I had 240 fillings.

As you can see, medicine in the United States is a pretty

complicated business. Regarding health care, there is one tip I can give you that I learned from my new American friends. They said, "You absolutely, positively, *cannot* get sick in this country unless you have medical insurance." Well, I'm not stupid. I'm not buying any.

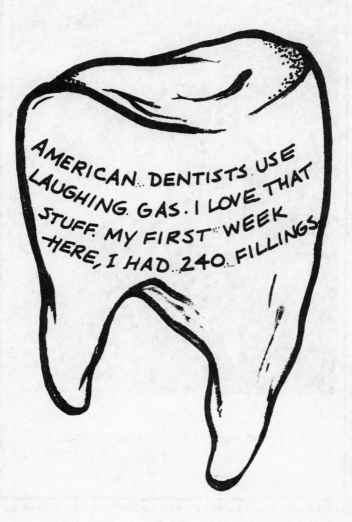

"I just bought my first American car . . . a Toyota!"

10

GETTING A CAR

or
I Think I'm Turning Japanese

"There's a *Ford* in your future!"

To most people, that means heading for a car dealer's showroom. (Of course, if you're a celebrity, it means you're heading for the Betty Ford Clinic.)

If you've been in this country for a while, you already know that the United States has perhaps the best system of transportation in the world. Even in Russia, we had heard of the incredible network of superhighways that crisscrosses the nation. Naturally, when I arrived in the U.S., I couldn't wait to experience these wonders of modern travel. I'll never forget my first trip on an American freeway. I was having the time of my life going everywhere, passing trucks and changing lanes, when all of a sudden a policeman stopped me and said, "You're supposed to be in a car."

In the Soviet Union I had a convertible car. It was called a bicycle. The most popular car in Russia is called a Lenin Continental . . . it seats eight prisoners (uncomfortably). I remember that when I was a teen-ager, every Saturday night I'd ask my father for the keys and he'd always say the same thing: "All right, son, but don't lose them, because someday we might get a car." In Russia I drove only once. My father let me borrow the family tank for my prom. I scored that night. We used to have a bumper sticker on it that said, "My other tank is a Chrysler."

One thing in Russia, they teach you to be a very safety-conscious driver. I would always use my seat belts, even if I was just driving around the Soviet Block. You never know when you might hit an Iron Curtain or be forced to make a sudden stop—like at the border!

I had often heard that Americans have love affairs with their cars, and I think that might be true. Once I was over at a friend's house and he was showing me his new convertible. He kept stroking the headlights and patting its rear end. When he said he was going to put the top down for me, I had to run home and take a cold shower! I was so excited that I started fantasizing about getting a car of my own. The only thing was, though, I didn't want a *used* one. Let's face it, there's the kind of car you'll take out for a joyride, and then there's the kind of car you'll want for the long haul.

Men aren't the only ones who view cars in strange ways. I have also heard some women say that the type of car a man drives is often a symbol of his virility. If that's really the case, I'm getting rid of my compact and investing in a stretch limo.

So, how do you go about finding that first car? There are many ways to approach this. Some people will tell you that one of the best ways to buy a car is through a private party. I went to a stag, a bar mitzvah, and a shower. I didn't find any good cars . . . but I did pick something up at the stag. What I would suggest instead is that you look in the classified ad section of your local newspaper. There you will find listings of people who are selling their cars. When I did this, the very first ad I looked at caught my eye: "74 LTD PS PB PW AC AT AM FM." I had no idea what it meant, but I figured any car with that many initials has got to be good! Then I saw it. I told the owner he was full of "BS." The next ad I called said: " '75 Chevy—Must Sacrifice." When I got there, he was setting the car on fire! Finally I saw a car that looked pretty good. The man said I could try it out, so I started it up and began backing out of his driveway. As they say in America, it really "purred like a kitten." After I apologized to the man for killing his cat, I went home.

If you have as much bad luck with the classifieds as I did, you might want to try a car lot, which is a place that has hundreds of cars and almost as many salesmen. These guys are better at following you around than the KGB! (Fortunately, car salesmen are easier to spot. If the KGB walked around in purple sportcoats, plaid pants, striped ties, and white belts, they would no longer be able to be *secret* police.) Your first time on a car lot you may feel lost and unsure of what to do, but watching how other customers act is not recommended. The first time I went to look at cars, I saw everybody kicking the tires, and I thought, "What an interesting way Americans have of testing their products." This theory did not make me a popular customer in the crystal department at Sears. (By the way, please contact me if you're looking for a forty-piece Waterford crystal vase.)

If you still are not sure whether to trust the salesman you're dealing with, here are a couple of tips that might help you steer clear of making an expensive mistake. Remember, he's probably trying to sell you a bad car if:

1. he offers to let you take it out for a "test push"

or

2. he says, "That's no tow truck. That's a hood ornament!"

Americans also use some unusual phrases when they talk about cars. For instance, the salesman told me he would show me something that had "a lot of balls," and "great rubber."

I asked, "Are you sure you're selling cars?"

He said, "Of course. What do I look like—a pimp?"

I thought to myself, "No, pimps dress better."

He bragged to me that this car could go 110 miles per hour. I wasn't impressed. Russian cars can go 200 m.p.h.—if you fill them with rocks and push them off a cliff!

Now, I didn't know a lot about cars when I went shopping, so a friend told me I should take someone with me. I did this, but it was a terrible idea. The girl said it was the worst date she had ever been on. What I now suggest is that you bring someone with you *who knows about cars.* You also have the right to take a car to a mechanic to have it checked out. When I found a car I was interested in, I took it to a nearby garage. The mechanic spent fifteen minutes looking it over, checking the engine and kicking the tires. I asked him, "Do you think I'm being cheated?" He said no and charged me $375. I left feeling much more secure.

I finally decided to buy the car, so I went back to the dealer to begin haggling. This means negotiating the price you will pay. It really is an art that requires quick thinking, nerves of steel, and a sound financial mind. I was ready. He made the first move. "The sticker price is $8,000," he said. I had to let him know that he wasn't dealing with a fool. I looked him square in the eye and replied, "How much without the sticker?"

Well, before you knew it we had a deal and I had bought my first American car: a Toyota, for $7,999!

"I want to be an organ donor."

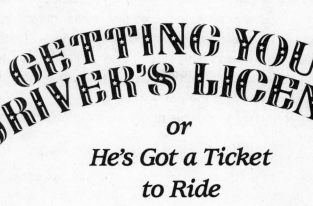

11

GETTING YOUR DRIVER'S LICENSE

or

He's Got a Ticket to Ride

All right, pull over! I know you're anxious to try out your new car, but you've forgotten the most important thing every driver must have. No, not a Baby on Board sign. I'm talking about a driver's license. In America, you need a license for just about everything: to practice medicine, to drive a car—even dogs need licenses, although I've never seen a dog driving. (Well, there was that one girl at the beach. . . .) Even when you get married, you must get a marriage license. (Shortly after that, the husband usually gets his hunting and fishing license.)

To get your driver's license, you must go to your local Department of Motor Vehicles. There you will find some of America's most pleasant, hardworking citizens—all waiting in line for a DMV employee to get back from his break. To avoid standing in this line, I suggest you do not go there during the employees' lunch hour, which usually runs from 9:00 A.M. to 5:00 P.M.

The first step toward getting your license is called the written exam. You will be given a piece of paper with questions about driving on it. This is a multiple-choice test, which means you pick the correct answer from four possible choices. (In the Soviet Union, the Russian government doesn't like to confuse its citizens, so they just give you three ways to answer: the right way, the wrong way, and the party way.)

Let me give you a few sample questions from an American driving test:

1. According to police statistics, what is the most expensive ticket given?
   A. speeding
   B. parking
   C. littering
   D. Policemen's Ball

The answer, of course, is D. If you argue about this ticket, you will get A, B, and C.

2. The DMV may refuse to issue you a license if you:
   A. lied on your license application.
   B. do not understand the traffic laws or signals.
   C. have a history of alcohol or drug abuse.
   D. attended the Ted Kennedy Driving School.

Once again, the correct answer is D. (This also will keep you from getting a lifeguard's license.)

3. Name the four leading causes of accidents.
   A. alcohol
   B. slippery roads
   C. recklessness
   D. that asshole who drives everywhere with his left-turn signal on

If you guessed D, you're right again.

After you've passed the written test, the next step is the road test. This is where you will drive your car accompanied by a DMV examiner, who will grade your driving ability. The first thing he will ask you to show him is the hand signals for left turn, right turn, and stop. Study these signals carefully. It's important that you do them *exactly* as shown in the manual. Otherwise . . . well, my left-hand signal was a little off, and the Italian examiner thought I was telling him to go suck a tailpipe. He responded by throwing me out of the car and showing me the hitchhiking signal—with the wrong finger!

Before you begin the road test, be sure to adjust all your equipment and make sure that everything is working properly. If you're not sure of the purpose of something, don't hesitate to ask. After driving for over two years, my father recently asked me, "What are those mirrors for?" (I immediately called Allstate Insurance and told them I needed a couple more hands.) Once you're out on the road, you will be judged on how you control the vehicle in residential areas, in crowded intersections, and on the freeway. (For women, there is an additional test where you must put eyeliner on at fifty-five miles per hour.) If you pass all these tests, you get your driver's license. The only thing left to do is to get your license picture taken by the DMV's professional photographer. They always try to make you look like a movie star—Ernest Borgnine!

You'll no doubt be very excited after getting your license, but let me give you a word of caution. A license does not mean you are an expert. You will still probably find yourself in some situations where you are not exactly sure what to do. For a long time I was confused about the right-of-way law. The driving book said: "At an intersection, the car on the right always gets to go first." One day I sat there for two hours before the car on the right showed up. But now I have ten years of driving experience and would not do such a silly thing. I only give the car on the right five minutes to show up . . . and then I find an alternate route.

A chapter on driving would not be complete without covering one last area. There is a saying in America: "Accidents will happen." Unfortunately, at some point you will probably be involved in a traffic accident. Naturally, should this occur, the most important thing to find out is that you and the other driver are all right. Remember, sometimes an injury from an auto accident won't show up for a day or two, so you should always be examined by a professional—your lawyer. It's amazing how many people walk into an attorney's office feeling fine, only to come out with a neck or back injury that otherwise might have gone unnoticed.

Your driver's license actually gives you the opportunity to do more than just drive. If you sign the card on the back of your license, you can become an organ donor. Now, I don't own an organ, but I told them they could definitely put me down for a clarinet. The officials explained to me that being an organ donor means you agree to let them take parts of your body if you should die. There is a similar program in Russia, only you don't have to agree, and they don't have to wait until you're dead!

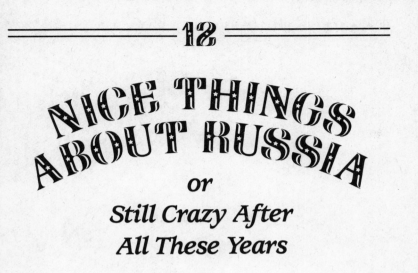

12

NICE THINGS ABOUT RUSSIA

or

Still Crazy After
All These Years

(continued on next page)

(continued on next page)

Just kidding. I guess there are a few nice things about Russia. For example, there's plenty of parking places, and always a policeman when you need one. And the Post Office is much faster—they read your mail over the phone!

"I like the American version of
roulette much better."

TRAVEL/ VACATION

or
Fifty Ways to Leave Your Country

You need a vacation!

"Vacation" is the word Americans use to describe going someplace different to have fun and get away from all their trials and tribulations. The English call it "holiday." In Russia, it's known as "defecting."

I know what you're thinking: "But Yakov, America's such a big place. How do I know where to spend my vacation?" Well, don't worry. I'm here to tell you where to go. You're right about America being a big place; so let's start out with a couple of basic tips. First, don't try to see it all in one day. Second, wear comfortable shoes. It took me quite a while to become an experienced vacationer, because traveling was not something you did much in Russia, at least not by *your* choice. Because we were not allowed to move freely, we used to approach our vacation time with a different attitude. We would brag about places we *couldn't* go. A typical vacation discussion sounded something like this:

ALEXEI: I can't go to Miami this year!

NIKOLAI: Miami? You call that a vacation? I can't go to *Paris!*

As a matter of fact, the only way to move in Russia is to marry someone from another city. That's why the divorce rate is so high. It's not that the people don't love each other, they just want to see the country. There is one vacation resort in the Soviet Union for the privileged: Club Red. For the rest of the citizens, there is an amusement park in Siberia called Dissident Land. When they take you for a ride, they don't bring you back.

Amusement parks make wonderful vacation trips in America. The best one of them all is Disneyland. My parents and I went there when we first moved to California. The first ride I wanted to go on was Space Mountain. But when we got there, my parents saw a long line of people going in and no one coming out and heard people screaming inside. My father said, "No thanks, we've seen this one before. We'll take another ride." Instead, we went to the souvenir stand. My parents got one look at the prices, started screaming, and headed back to Space Mountain.

Las Vegas is a very popular vacation spot for people who like gambling. (Personally, I enjoy the American version of roulette much more. You only end up with a hole in your wallet.) There are so many wonderful games to play. I was having fun at the blackjack table until the woman I was sitting next to said, "Hit me! Hit me!" So I did. (This is where the police taught me a new meaning for the word "busted.") It can be tough on a foreigner in Las Vegas, though. You see, in English they sometimes use the same word for two completely different things. This caused me to have a very embarrassing moment at the crap table! Then I went to an Elvis impersonator's show and found a third use for the word.

Being new to the United States, you might want to visit the nation's capital, Washington, D.C. It's not only fun, it's also educational. When I went to Washington, I ate at a restaurant that names all of its meals after famous political figures. For breakfast, I had a Khadaffi and Carter. That's flakes and nuts.

Being in Washington really gives you a chance to see how the American government works. I was particularly interested in seeing Congress in action. Unfortunately, when I got there they were in recess . . . so I went back later for milk and cookies!

Whenever I go to New York City, I always stop by and see this woman who still carries the torch for me—the Statue of Liberty. New York is also the city where I had my first experience with freedom of choice. A man came up to me and said, "Your money or your life!" I'm kidding! I love New York! However, it is an expensive place to visit. I was walking through Times Square and a girl told me she would screw me for fifty dollars. I replied, "Fifty dollars? In *Red* Square I could get screwed for nothing!"

Being on vacation doesn't mean you have to stay in one place. If you want to see some of the country and be entertained at the same time, there is a unique trip you can take on a train where you will witness a murder and try to figure out who did it. They call it a Murder Mystery Train. In Russia, it's called a commuter.

If you prefer traveling on the open sea, you can always go on a cruise. These luxury ships sail all over the world and make frequent stops for sightseeing, shopping, and icebergs. While on the ship, there are many fun activities for you to participate in. I once did something called "para-sailing." For people who don't know what para-sailing is, a parachute is strapped to your back and you are put on a platform which is floating behind the boat. The boat pulls you, and suddenly you shoot up two hundred feet in the air! I realized that all there was between me and instant death was a little strap between my legs. I did great . . . but I should have worn brown pants. At one point up there I actually saw God and He spoke to me! He said, "Yakov . . . you should have worn brown pants."

Now, I know in many of your native countries, nude beaches are a very common and normal thing. We did not have nude beaches in Russia, and I thanked the Lord every day for it. There are a few nude beaches in America. I just happened to accidentally stumble across one . . . after searching extensively for three weeks, climbing over mountains. When I took my first walk down the beach, I became very happy to be in America. As a matter of fact, it was hard to conceal my happiness! I guess I'm just a naturally happy guy, by and large. But after I'd spent a while inconspicuously leering at all the women on the beach, something strange happened (no, not that!). The novelty of seeing all these naked women wore off and I found myself looking at them and thinking, "Hmmm, I wonder how she'd look in a tight sweater."

California is another great place to visit. I go to San Diego a lot because I have a friend at Camp Pendleton who works there—as a spy. (I'm kidding. He got fired.) But it is for my adopted home of Los Angeles that I can give you the best vacation tips. When visiting L.A., you must go to Hollywood and see Mann's Chinese Theater. You'll love looking at all the hand- and foot-prints in the sidewalk. I figured that this is the latest advancement in citizen identification—the FBI must require all Americans to leave their prints and a clever saying in wet cement. And what would a trip to California be without seeing a TV show taping? The first time I went, I couldn't believe all the cameras, microphones, and people watching—it looked just like a Soviet apartment.

No matter where you travel in America, there are always plenty of nice places to stay that have every feature you could want—and even a few you don't want. I took my parents to Hawaii once, and the hotel we stayed at provided closed-circuit X-rated movies. They charged six dollars a film. Now, my father thought they were free, so he figured he could watch them and no one would know. When we checked out, I got the bill and said, "Dad? Adult entertainment . . . $180? Are you okay?" He smiled and said, "Yep!" I asked him why he'd been watching these movies and he told me it was to learn English. So I asked him what he had learned and he replied, "Oh baby, baby! Make it hurt!"

VACATIONING IN NEW YORK CITY, YOU WILL TRULY EXPERIENCE THE FREEDOM OF CHOICE – YOUR MONEY OR YOUR LIFE!

"No wonder there are so many
burglaries in America."

14

CRIME

or
Killing Me Softly with His Gun

Crime is a problem that can be found in every country of the world. Here in the U.S. it is called by several different names: The Mob, The Underworld, and The Family. In the Soviet Union, crime is called by only one name: the government. Actually, crime in the USA really isn't any worse than anywhere else in the world, but it is more interesting. I was amazed when I heard about things like white-collar crime and blue-collar crime. I thought to myself, "What a country! A dress code for criminals." Even the police must be sharp dressers, because I read all the time that they're preparing to "formally" charge some criminal. Another thing that may surprise you is how important it is to always have an alibi in the United States. At any time, an American may ask you if you remember where you were the morning that Pearl Harbor was attacked, or what you were doing the day President Kennedy was assassinated. Luckily, I can prove I was out of the country both times.

Police departments, like those in the United States, are created to protect you and keep you safe. As a matter of fact, thanks to them, Americans have many wonderful things we never had in the Soviet Union. Like warning shots. I think they're great. In Russia, the police don't shoot up in the air. They shoot you! . . . and that's warning for the next guy.

Soviet police are much different from their American counterparts. For instance, the Russian police have a Missing Persons Department; that's where they decide which persons are going to be missing. Of course, this doesn't mean that Soviet police are inhuman. A Russian cop is always willing to give you a break—usually your leg.

In both nations, people are always interested in what their rights are. Like here in the United States, you have "the right to remain silent." In the USSR it's not a right, it's an order! Also in America you are "innocent until proven guilty." In Russia, you are "guilty until executed"!

Perhaps you've heard stories about Russian citizens who claim to have been given a ten-year jail sentence when they were completely innocent. Well, I can tell you that is an absolute lie. If you're innocent, you only get *five* years. I don't know if you've noticed or not, but the Communist government rarely sentences anyone to "life." They don't like to make promises they can't keep.

It might take you a while to completely understand how the courts in America work. Lawyers are particularly puzzling. Now, apparently all you have to do in the United States to become a lawyer is "pass the bar." That's why there aren't that many attorneys in the Soviet Union: Russians just can't pass a bar.

Some lawyers here seem a little kinky to me. I needed some legal work done recently, and a lawyer told me that if I paid him

$150, he'd "make some motions for me with his briefs." I turned him down. I figured for $150, I could get a girl to make some motions for me (without any underwear at all).

Now, I've kidded a little about lawyers here, but actually I have a great deal of respect and admiration for them. If it weren't for the legal profession we never would have had things like civil rights, personal freedom, and Perry Mason reruns.

The more you learn about crime here, the more complicated you may find the terminology. For instance, there was a story on the eleven-o'clock news the other night about a man who committed second-degree murder and first-degree murder. Now, I don't mind a guy continuing his education. I just don't want him getting his Master's on me!

Also, a lot of people here think the solution to violent crime in this country is strict gun control. I don't know if that is the answer or not, but in the Soviet Union, the Communist government has had gun control for years. Guns control everything!

To me, most Americans seem to ignore several obvious ways to protect themselves against criminals. First, you will often read about a murder and the police will say that they found the body in a "pool of blood." Now, I'm not going to say that it was the guy's own fault that he got killed, but I can think of safer places to go swimming.

And though Americans claim to be very concerned about the crime problem, they do some pretty bizarre things. Recently I was driving down the street and I saw this big sign in front of someone's home that said, OPEN HOUSE. I thought to myself, "No wonder there are so many burglaries here."

The best thing you can probably do is try to pick a home in a fairly good area. But no matter how careful you are, there are no guarantees. I chose an apartment in a section of town that was supposedly quite nice. I even asked the building's manager if it was safe and he said not to worry because they had a neighborhood watch. I didn't understand what that meant until I got mugged . . . and the whole neighborhood watched.

The bottom line here is that crime is the second fastest growing industry in the United States. The first is Amway, and to tell you the truth, I think I prefer crime. It's more honest!

"I like this middle of the road music."

15

MUSIC

or
Tanks for the Memories

It's better to be a hip American than a Red Square.

I love American rock music. It's hot! It's cool! It's bad! It's good! It's real! It's unreal! It's . . . Oh, I'm sorry. Sometimes I get carried away with this hip American rock-and-roll language. Let me explain what it all means. If something is "hot," this means it is really exciting and great. On the other hand, if something is "cool," this means it is really exciting and great. Now, if something is "bad," well, what this means is that it is really exciting and— I think you get the idea.

Now MTV is Music Television—a TV channel where you can watch rock musicians sing, dance, and stick their faces too close to the camera twenty-four hours a day. In Russia, they also have MTV—Military Television! My favorite video was the one where all the Soviet politicians got together and sang, "We Arm the World." (The flip side of the record was "These Boots Are Made for Marching.")

One of the toughest things to get used to will be all the different names of rock bands. When you first hear of groups called Ratt, The Grateful Dead, or Twisted Sister, the names sound pretty silly, until you *see* the guys in these groups. Then it starts to make sense.

You might be surprised to know that there is rock music in the Soviet Union, but you will not be surprised to know that they steal a lot from American music. We had folk groups like Peter, Paul, and Olga singing, "If I Had a Hammer and a Sickle" and "This Land *Was* Your Land." One of the best Soviet rock bands is The Rolling Tanks. It's a heavy metal sound. But they're never home. They're always touring all over the world. They just got back from Afghanistan singing, "You Can't Always Get What You Want." My friends in Russia tell me the most popular group now is Huey Lewis and No News!

While living in your home countries, many of you probably received American rock records with lyrics translated into your native language. In Russia, they used to change the words entirely. The government did not want the songs to excite the youth, so they gave them much tamer lyrics. For instance, in the Soviet Union, "Let's Go Crazy" was retitled "Why Don't We Go Slightly Abnormal?" and "Born to Run" is known as "Conceived to Walk Fast." It makes it a little tougher to sing along. And they took the ZZ Top song "She's Got Legs . . . and She Knows How to Use Them" and changed it to "She's Got Facial Hair . . . and She Knows How to Groom It."

The late Elvis Presley was probably the most popular American rock singer. He was even well known in Russia. We used one of his songs for my high school prom theme—"Jailhouse Rock." Elvis, as you know, is the King of Rock and Roll. I don't think there is a queen . . . unless you count Michael Jackson. There is a Prince, however. A typical Prince concert consists of half-naked women, dirty talk, and lots of sex—and that's in the audience. I'm so glad my parents brought me with them! What a country!

Last year, I went to see Bruce Springsteen. There were ninety thousand people gathered in one place raising their fists in the air and shouting about the USA. Of course, I'd seen this before, but this time no one was burning any flags!

In America, Bruce Springsteen is known as The Boss. I started thinking, "If I had a great nickname, maybe I could become a rock star too." I made a list of possible names: The Godfather of Soul, Mr. Dynamite, The Hardest-Working Man in Show Business, and Mr. Sex Machine. Then I found out that they were all taken—by James Brown! This did not seem fair to me at all, but I was new here and didn't want to make trouble. I decided to pick a really silly nickname that no one else could possibly have—Sting.

A word of warning to new immigrants. Rock music is not a good way to try to learn English. You can't imagine the embarrassment and pain I went through when I used to start conversations by saying, "I want a man with a slow hand" or "You make me feel like a natural woman."

Once you start to develop favorite singers, you'll want to know how their latest records are doing. American television provides you with many shows that keep track of this information and present it every week. In Russia, we had only one show like this: "Anti-American Bandstand." I always got nervous during the "weekly countdown." When they say a song is "number 2 with a bullet," you better get out and buy it!

There are so many different categories of American music: pop, which is my father's favorite; jazz, which is Bill Cosby's favorite (actually I just wanted to mention Bill Cosby's name somewhere in the book); and punk, which you have to stick a pin in your nose to listen to. That way you don't think about the pain in your ears. In the Soviet Union, we also have people who shave parts of their head and color their hair orange ... we call them mentally ill. While in an office building recently, I heard what Americans call "elevator music." It really brought me down. Another kind of music I discovered is called "middle of the road." While listening to one of those records, I almost got hit by a truck! One of the newest forms of music in the Soviet Union is called "country eastern." The biggest hit song of this type is "Salt Miner's Daughter" by Loretta Lenin.

Buying records in America is very easy. You just go to your local record shop or department store. Even supermarkets and gas stations sell records (although I don't advise you to go to these places unless you're looking for albums by Telly Savalas and Leonard Nimoy). In Russia, I belonged to the KGB Record Club. For just one penny, they send you thirteen recordings of your own telephone conversations! One more tip: don't buy records advertised on TV in America, especially by singers you don't know. I spent $29.95 on a triple album called *Connie Francis's Greatest Hits.* Guess "who's sorry now?"

If you don't want to spend money on records, then you can just listen to your car radio until you find some music that appeals to you. American radio is great, but I wish they would be a little more careful when they choose a name. There is a station in San Diego called KGB-FM. I was driving along one night and the announcer said, "This is KGB-FM. It's ten o'clock. We know where you are." I almost crashed into the car in front of me!

"MIDDLE OF THE ROAD"
MUSIC CAN BE DANGEROUS.
WHILE LISTENING TO ONE
OF THOSE ALBUMS, I ALMOST
GOT HIT BY A TRUCK!

"Drinks are on the house."

16

HOLIDAYS

or
I'm Dreaming of a Red Christmas

appy Holidays! Americans love holidays. They're very special days which give people a chance to commemorate famous dates in history, to honor those who have made this country great, and to score a three-day weekend off from work. Every month of the year has some sort of holiday except for August, which I don't understand, because Richard Nixon resigned August 8, 1974. This sounded to me like it was a cause for celebration. (Maybe you should write to your congressman to consider making August 8 "So Long Dick Day.")

I am going to run down a few of the new holidays you will be celebrating, tell you what they're about, and how most Americans observe them.

New Year's Day: This is one holiday I haven't completely figured out yet. It marks the first day of the new year, but as far as celebrating, all Americans seem to do is lie in bed with an ice pack on their head, moan, and drink Alka-Seltzer.

Washington's Birthday: All over the United States, you will see signs saying: GEORGE WASHINGTON SLEPT HERE. Obviously, this is how he became Father of His Country. This date also marks the beginning of an event that has become an institution in America—The George Washington Birthday Furniture Sale at J.C. Penney.

St. Patrick's Day: A day in which people wear weird clothes, get drunk, and throw up on their shoes. In America, it's called St. Patrick's Day. In Russia, it's called Tuesday . . . and Wednesday . . . and Thursday . . .

Mother's Day: A special day to show your mother just how much you love her. A popular American tradition is to give your mother breakfast in bed. I tried it once, but it wasn't easy getting that mattress and box spring into the kitchen.

July 4th: Also known as the Fourth of July. This occasion commemorates the signing of the Declaration of Independence. On this very important day in history, Americans like to get together with friends, barbecue hamburgers and hot dogs, and drink beer. Many towns will have a fireworks display where you sit outside with about thirty thousand other people, look up at the sky, and say "oooh" and "aaah." Russian fireworks are different. They put you against a wall and yell, "Fire." (It works.) Also held on this day is the Fourth of July Furniture Blow-Out Sale at J.C. Penney.

Secretaries' Day: If you are employed at a business where you have a secretary, this is the day you reward her for all her loyalty and hard work. You might take her to lunch, give her the afternoon off . . . or have your wife run out at lunchtime to pick her up a scarf.

Labor Day: Not to be confused with the Russian holiday Hard Labor Day. I used to think that Labor Day was to honor the mother of the Osmond family, the Jacksons' mother, and Mrs. Lopez down the street, but actually it is to pay tribute to the country's work force. Because Labor Day is to honor them, Americans like to spend the day with friends, barbecuing and drinking beer. This day also marks the beginning of off-season rates for hotels, the Jerry Lewis telethon, and the Labor Day Furniture Liquidation Sale at J.C. Penney.

Columbus Day: In honor of Christopher Columbus, the man who discovered Ohio.

Halloween: Americans dress up in expensive costumes, scary makeup, and walk through the streets at night . . . just to get a Snickers bar!

Thanksgiving: A day on which Americans give thanks for all the wonderful blessings that have enriched their lives. They do this by eating a Thanksgiving dinner, which is a tradition that started with the Pilgrims and the Indians. It was at this historic dinner that one Indian was overheard saying, "Well, there goes the nation!"

THANKSGIVING IS A GREAT AMERICAN HOLIDAY. I REALLY LIKE PARADES WITHOUT MISSILES.

"Here's where I get most of my material."

17

POLITICS/ GOVERNMENT

or
You're Nobody till Somebody Bribes You

ow many Russians does it take to screw up Poland?" That won first prize in the Soviet Union's Best Political Joke contest. You probably noticed that there's no punch line. The government gave the guy who told it twenty years to think of one.

Living in America, you will be free to make jokes about politics or any other subject you want, although you might get some disagreement on this from Earl Butz, James Watt, or Al Campanis. Being able to tell a political joke is another example of the great freedom of speech you will have in America. In Russia now, because of the new openness (*Glasnost*), they also have freedom of speech, but in America you have freedom *after* you speak. It's a nice little feature.

It's very important to use your privilege to vote in this country. You not only make your voice heard on important political matters, but you also can get lots of free bumper stickers. Registering to vote in your first election is exciting—and mystifying. When I went to register, the woman asked me, "What party would you like to join?" I said, "Not this again!"

To save you some time, let me explain that the American government operates on a two-party system, the Republicans and the Democrats. In Russia, they also have two parties—the living and the dead. Voting for the first time in America was one of the biggest thrills of my life. Not that I haven't voted before. In Russian elections, they used secret ballots, but they were secret from us!

If you are from Poland, you will play a very important part in American politics. For some reason, every politician in this country wants to do well with the Poles. Please don't take it personally, however, if a certain candidate says that he doesn't believe in the Poles. This just means he knows he is going to get his ass kicked in the election.

You can learn a lot about the candidates by watching televised debates. I enjoy American debates much more than Soviet debates because there are two people instead of one! If you don't want to take the time to study the important issues, but still want to make your voice heard, you should consider running for office yourself. Or you can just vote for whatever candidates have the most celebrities campaigning for them. (Millions of Americans use Jane Fonda in this way. Whoever she votes for, they vote against.) When I see Americans treating their privilege to vote in such a lighthearted manner, it really gets me mad. Here's what I go through when deciding who gets my vote: First, I learn all about the candidates, then I see how they stand on the issues. I look at their past records and then vote for whoever was the best guest star on "Miami Vice."

You are given many rights and freedoms living in America. In return, the government expects certain things from you.

After I was sworn in as a citizen, I immediately had requests for interviews from NBC, CBS, and IRS. Paying taxes is the duty of every American. That's why it's important to find yourself a good accountant. All Russian citizens have their taxes done by U.S.S. and R. Block. And they don't have to give you any reasons! The first time I went to an American accountant, he looked over all of my information and told me, "You're in the red." I said, *"Déjà vu."* I definitely prefer the American tax system to the Soviets'. I'll take a loophole over a bullet hole any day!

As Americans, you will find that your government also keeps you very well informed through published reports, interviews, and Sam Donaldson. In many countries, the governments never give the people accurate information. For example, when the Chernobyl nuclear disaster happened in Russia, Soviet officials told the people they were trying to make soft ice cream and things just got out of hand. When Russian citizens questioned these announcements, the government continued to lie, saying they had called Chernobyl and received nothing but "glowing reports." (They didn't care that now every Soviet cloud has a nuclear lining.)

The biggest political problem you will hear about most often in this country is Soviet-American relations, particularly the nuclear freeze. I don't know if this situation will ever be settled, because to the Russians, a "nuclear freeze" means moving the missiles to Siberia. Some progress is being made, however, at the summit talks between Mr. Gorbachev and President Reagan. Gorbachev has made it clear that he is in favor of disarmament. That's why he disarmed Poland, Czechoslovakia, and Afghanistan!

I followed these issues very closely through the newspapers and TV, and when Gorbachev asked Reagan to get rid of the

MX or Trident missiles, I actually wrote a letter to the president, giving him my opinion that he should get rid of the MX rather than the Trident because "four out of five Americans prefer Trident." I think the next time I will write him to say that I don't like Star Wars—I enjoyed *Return of the Jedi* much more.

"Hmm. So that's what you call an overhead smash."

SPORTS

or
We're in the Money

Sports in the United States are a lot more fun than the ones in Russia. In the Soviet Union the only sports we had were the Olympics, and they weren't much fun because the government puts enormous pressure on the athletes to win. For instance, if a male athlete loses, he becomes a female athlete. And it hurts!

Like here in the U.S., there is also a steroid problem among the athletes in Russia—the government has a problem convincing them to take them. Actually, steroids don't work on Soviet athletes anymore . . . now they have to take "asteroids". The only side effect is that the women grow a third breast. And personally, I kind of liked it.

What I'm going to do here is give you a short description of some of the more popular sports in America so that you can do what every true-blue, red-blooded American sports fan does—get drunk and complain about the players' salaries.

BASEBALL

Baseball is often considered the Great American National Pastime and is a wonderful escape. (This is not to be confused with the Great Russian National Pastime, which is simply to escape!) They don't play baseball in the Soviet Union because there, no one is safe. And the Communist government wouldn't allow anyone to hit a home run. As soon as the ball crossed the fence . . . they'd shoot it down. Besides, if they did decide to start playing baseball there, the Russian army would want to add three more bases—strategically located and for defensive purposes only.

I love watching baseball here in America and have really gotten into following some of the players' statistics. My favorite pitcher currently has quite a record—18 wins, 6 losses, and 3 arrests. You will probably also enjoy baseball, particularly once you realize what incredible athletes these players are. I am still amazed every time I hear on the radio that a player has managed to catch several "fly balls." How do they see those little things? (This explains why they all wear gloves.)

To further complicate things for you, baseball terminology is often used in many different ways in the English language. For a while, I kept hearing a lot of baseball terms that relate to dating. If you ask a girl to go out and she says no, they say you've "struck out." But if you're lucky, you'll get to "first base." Just be careful, because if you get her pregnant, you're not a "free agent" anymore. (Lately, I haven't had many dates, so I've been spending a lot of time alone in the batting cage taking "practice swings.") But some of the most confusing phrases are in the rules of the game itself. For example, they say, "If you have four balls, you walk." Of course, you walk. How are you going to run with four balls? You walk proud!

FOOTBALL

Football was a difficult sport for me to grasp at first. I don't understand why grown men would want to bend over and touch each other . . . well, maybe I do. Football is often criticized as one of the most violent sports in America. And apparently Dallas is one of the worst offenders. If you don't believe it, all you have to do is look in the sports section of your local newspaper. You'll see headlines like COWBOYS WIPE OUT BUFFALO! and COWBOYS KILL REDSKINS! Now, it's not bad enough that they've made the poor buffalos extinct—they've got to start picking on those Indians again.

Football is one sport that would never be popular in the Soviet Union. As soon as the Russian fans heard that the quarterback was going to throw the bomb, they'd run out of the stadium.

As you can see, football also has its share of confusing phrases. For example, their world championship game. They call it the Super Bowl. For the longest time, I thought the Super Bowl was something in Superman's bathroom.

BASKETBALL

Basketball is a very popular sport here in the United States, and you will immediately notice that the players are all very tall. If you would like to play the game, many cities have an Over-25 League. I never joined because I'm not even over 5'8".

This sport is also played in the Soviet Union, but the rules are adhered to much more strictly there. For example, if a Russian player goes out of bounds . . . he is shot! It cuts down on a lot of unnecessary game delays.

To better learn how to play this American game, the Soviets invited the National Basketball Association to send a team to the USSR for an exhibition game. Unfortunately, the NBA chose the team from Houston; when they told the Russian government that the Rockets would be arriving shortly, they almost started World War Three! I hear that now they're going to send over the Boston Celtics . . . because Reagan wants to give Gorbachev "the Bird."

HOCKEY

Now, here's a game that at least I understood before I came to the U.S. Who could forget the Russian hockey team that got beaten so soundly by the Americans in the 1980 Olympics? (They're still practicing in some cold place where there's plenty of ice.) Because of that defeat, the Russians instituted many changes in their international sports programs. The biggest change is that now the Soviets hold Olympic trials *after* the games. And instead of needing a coach, athletes need a lawyer.

Fortunately, hockey here is not taken quite so seriously. But it is a little difficult to see why the athletes work so hard to get into the playoffs. I understand that all the championship team wins is the Stanley Cup. I mean, what is Stanley supposed to wear? And the really disgusting thing is that they all drink champagne out of it!

HORSE RACING

The Sport of Kings.

DRAG RACING

The Sport of Queens.

GOLF

Recently I took up golf. I was told that before I could go out and play it, I would need a set of clubs and a caddy. The clubs were reasonable enough, but I couldn't afford the caddy . . . so I got a Pontiac instead. Golf is a challenging game that requires catlike reflexes, keen hand-to-eye coordination, and strong, steady nerves. If you don't have all of those skills, that windmill hole will beat you every time.

Actually, I did try golfing for real last summer. Scoring is very difficult in this sport. I was told by my instructor to try to hit a birdie or at least an eagle. I didn't do either, but backing out with the golf cart, I did run over a pigeon. My first time out, I had a score of 73, and I didn't even play a second hole. Because of my golfing ability, they gave me the highest handicap in the country club. It was a little embarrassing, but at least I got to park in all those blue spaces.

Golfers really know how to make a sport enjoyable. My first time out on the course, I stumbled on the ball-washing machine. I said to myself, "What a country!" But it's hard to stay on top of that goddamn thing. I think I'll stick with showers.

I also saw another wonderful thing there. They have a sign that says, REGISTER YOUR BALLS HERE. I thought to myself, "What a country club! You lose your balls, and they send them back to you."

CROSS-COUNTRY SPORTS

The Soviet government has a proven record of success in the area of cross-country sports . . . cross Poland, cross Czechoslovakia, cross Afghanistan. Generally, cross-country sports come under the heading of track and field events and are very popular in America. Here is a short list of some that you may want to try:

HIGH JUMP: You jump high.
LONG JUMP: You jump long.
BROAD JUMP: Don't get excited, it's not what you think.

BOWLING

This is truly a sport that you will never see in Russia, because the Communists would never allow a strike. The surprising thing about bowling in America is that the rewards are so extravagant. I recently watched a game where the announcer said that the bowlers were playing for a "sixty-thousand-dollar purse." Now, those players may think that's great, but how are they going to afford the shoes to match?

POLO

Who cares?

TENNIS

Tennis is a sport that many people believe will be in the Olympics very soon. For that reason, the Soviet Union is trying to get its athletes to learn to play the game. The biggest obstacle is getting a Russian citizen to voluntarily go onto the "court." And the Communist party has changed a few of the rules to try to speed up the learning process. For example, in Russian tennis, if you question any of the line judge's calls, he will give you a one-point penalty—and a prison sentence!

SURFING

Russians don't surf. In the Soviet Union, "Hang Ten" has a completely different meaning.

In short, you should enjoy many of the American sports that are available to you. While I like most all of them, I'm really looking forward to the 1988 Olympics. But I don't think the Russians will be going to South Korea. You see, a Korean airline wants to sponsor their trip.

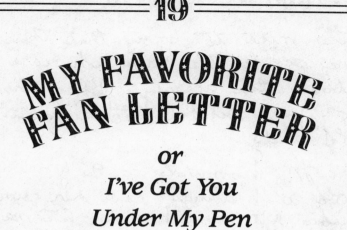

MY FAVORITE FAN LETTER

or

I've Got You
Under My Pen

Being in show business, I get a lot of mail from people who have seen me perform. Here is my favorite fan letter.

Dear Mr. Smirnoff,

God bless you for the beautiful radio I won at the senior citizen's raffle where you performed.

I am 84 years old and I live in a retirement home. My people are all gone and it's nice to know that there are people like you who care about the elderly. Bless you for your kindness to a forgotten old lady.

My roommate is 95 years old and always had her own radio but would never let me listen to it. The other day her radio fell and broke into a million pieces. It was awful and she asked if she could listen to mine, and I said eat shit and die.

Sincerely,
Edna Johnson

A Few Thousand Words About the Author

or
Please Release Me, Let Me Go

Whenever I am performing at various clubs and colleges around the United States, I like to open the floor for questions. (In Russia, you ask a question and they open the floor.) People are always curious about life in the Soviet Union, how I became a professional comedian, and whether I really drink Lite Beer.

Let me go back to the beginning of my life. It was my parents' wedding night. An empty bottle of vodka lay on the floor next to the bed. Balalaika music played softly in the background as they gazed into each other's eyes . . . maybe I'm going too far back.

Let's jump ahead. I was born in a log cabin in Kentucky . . . Wait a minute. That's not my life. That's Abraham Lincoln's! Sorry, I guess it's because me and Lincoln both have beards.

Seriously, I was born in the Soviet Union in the city of Odessa, which is just south of Dallas. I was a typical Russian baby—hungry, cold, and afraid. Fear is something every Soviet citizen acquires early. It comes in mother's milk. At the age of six months, I had already learned to talk. I wasn't a genius. The KGB *made* me talk!

Soon it was time for me to go to school. I went where every Russian child goes . . . the Little Red Schoolhouse. I really enjoyed school—playing games like Dodge Bomb and Hide and Stay Hidden. And every year on the first day of school we always had to write a composition called "What I Did on My Summer Invasion." But I was not your average Russian student. My high school class voted me "Most Likely to Be an American."

By the time I got out of high school, I had already started performing comedy around the Soviet Union. Many people are surprised to hear we have comedians in Russia, but they are there. They are *dead,* but they are there. Performers were very limited as to what they could say on stage. Before I could tell a joke in public, I had to send all my material to the local Department of Jokes. They would censor the material and send it to Moscow, where there is a big Department of Jokes—called the Politburo.

Once your act is approved, you have to stick to it. You cannot improvise. For instance, if someone heckles you, you can't say, "Your mother wears army boots," because she probably does. And she will hurt you! You really have to be careful what jokes you tell. If you say, "Take my wife, please," when you get home—she is gone!

You also are not allowed to make jokes about politics, sex, or religion—which leaves you with topics like buttons and fish. For instance, "Two baby seals walk into a bar and ask for a Canadian Club on the rocks." Pretty funny, huh? But there is one good thing about doing comedy in Russia. You've got a captive audience—they're not going anywhere!

A few years later, I finally got a job performing on a Soviet cruise ship, *The Love Barge.* It was there that I started meeting people from outside the USSR. They were having so much more fun than a Russian audience, and I figured it was just because they had eaten before the show. Then I realized it was because they were free. I knew it was time to make my move. After applying for an exit visa, some strange things happened to me. The KGB came one night, dragged me to their interrogation room, and asked me if I really wanted to leave Russia. I said, "No, I'm just doing a project on stress."

A few nights later, I was sound asleep when there was a knock on my door at 3:00 A.M. "Who is it?" I asked. "Mailman," a deep voice replied. I opened the door and there were two guys in trench coats. One of them asked me, "Why do you want to go to America?" I answered, "Because in America, they don't deliver your mail at 3:00 A.M.!" The following week, some government officials came to a small nightclub where I was performing. After seeing my show, they came backstage and said, "You can go now." Actually, I had it all planned. I did Pee-wee Herman's act!

My parents and I left Russia together. (We had a good travel agent.) We boarded an American luxury airliner for the first time. Soviet planes are much different—the rest rooms are outside. (It's a bitch if you're facing the wrong way.) As we prepared for takeoff, we held hands and smiled. We had never been happier. But our happiness soon turned to confusion when the stewardess announced that we should "bring our seats all the way forward." I realized I had no tools! Those things are bolted to the floor!

Then I had to go to the bathroom. I went in there and there was a sign over the toilet that said, NO FOREIGN OBJECTS ALLOWED. I panicked. This was a *twelve-hour flight!* I've always felt sorry for whoever used that cologne dispenser after me.

Once we landed, I had to go to immigration. Through the interpreter, they asked me what I wanted to do in America. I told them I wanted to be a comedian. I got the biggest laugh I ever had. I said to myself, "I'm doing great!"

While going through customs, some German shepherds started to sniff my luggage. When I asked what they were doing, I was told they were checking to see if I had any drugs. I had heard of *people* hooked on drugs, but dogs? (In Russia, the only drugs they have are downers. We call them bullets. Boy, do they mellow you out!) I really didn't know anything about drugs, but people were always telling me I should try them. So I tried Ex-Lax. I wasn't getting high, I was sitting real low! Then I tried acid and burned my lips. For six months, I was taking Midol. It was the worst period of my life! After all those experiences, it's very easy for me to "Just Say No!"

After living in New York a while, my parents and I decided to move to California, where there would be more opportunity for me, the weather is great, plus we would live three hours longer. While driving out west, we got to see a lot of this beautiful country. We spent one night in Cleveland. We really felt at home in Cleveland—so we had to escape again! (Just kidding.) Actually, I only make fun of Cleveland because all Americans do. Every country has one city that everybody makes fun of. For example, in Russia we used to make fun of Cleveland. Honestly, though, if I had only a year to live, I would spend it in Cleveland because it would feel like an eternity.

When we ultimately got to L.A., I set out to start my show-business career. Show business in America is different from what I was used to. Here you have to find an agent. In Russia, the agent always finds you. I looked through the newspapers to find some places I could perform. Every comedy club had an Open Mike Night, but I couldn't find one with an Open

Yakov Night. I finally found an ad for an Amateur Night. Perfect! In Russia, like all of their Olympic athletes, I was considered an amateur because I was paid for performing. Naturally, my parents were worried about my chances of succeeding because of the odds against me. Every time I would talk about being a comedian, my mother would shake her head and say, "We'll see."

I decided to go to the club that night just to watch the other comedians. While listening to their acts, I was amazed at the freedom of speech they had. They would even say, "I hate Reagan." I couldn't believe they were criticizing their country's leader. Of course, in Russia we were allowed to do that too. We could say "I hate Reagan!" I started to spend more time hanging around comedy clubs so I could watch and learn from America's best performers. I was very impressed with Richard Pryor and what a great human being he was, because in his act he was always mentioning his mother. (As my English got better, however, I realized he was talking about a different kind of "mother"!)

After years of working and practicing, things finally started to happen. Before I knew it, I was getting parts in movies and television shows. I even did Dr. Ruth (not her, the show). That was very embarrassing, because all she wanted to talk about was sex.

Even when I told my parents of all these wonderful things, and I made enough money to buy them a house, my mother would just shake her head and say, "We'll see."

Then I received the phone call that I had always dreamed about. I was asked to perform for the President of the United States. I couldn't believe it. They told me I would be performing in front of President Reagan's cabinet and I said, "Great! I've always wanted to see Nancy's china."

When the big night came, I was very nervous. I figured if the president didn't like me, I'd never work this country again. Fortunately, the show went great and my picture wound up in all the newspapers with President Reagan.

When I arrived back in Los Angeles, I was approached to be a regular character in a TV series that would be called "What a Country!" I immediately called my mother to tell her the news. She said, "Great! When can we put in the pool?"

I said, "We'll see."

The End of the Book

Well, you finally made it to the end of the book (or you're looking through it in the store and want to see how many pages there are). I hope you enjoyed reading it. I tried to cover a lot of topics, to guide you through your new life in these United States, while still leaving enough subjects open for a sequel if this thing sells big. I also should warn you not to take too seriously any of my suggestions on how to act in this country. I can't afford to bail you all out!

The publisher tells me that this book will be coming out around Thanksgiving. Thanksgiving is my favorite American holiday. I really like parades without missiles. (I'll take Bullwinkle over a tank any day!)

Now, when Thanksgiving in America was first explained to me, I said, "Wait, it doesn't make sense. I mean, for every freedom and all the opportunities you have here, the only thing you've got to say is 'thanks'?" It just didn't seem like it was enough.

My parents and I had our first Thanksgiving dinner in a little apartment in New York, and we joined hands and my father said a prayer for good food and our health, and then something happened. . . . Instead of releasing our hands, we couldn't let go. We kept holding on to each other tighter and tighter, as we realized we were together and we were free. Here we were, three grown people looking for a way we could possibly show our appreciation, and we couldn't.

Now I know what it is. It's "thanks."

America. What a country!